TEN TO TAKE HER HOME

TEN TO TAKE
HER HOME

The Life and Times of RDF

by

R. DEREK FINLAY

The Memoir Club

First published in 2006 by
The Memoir Club
Stanhope Old Hall
Stanhope
Weardale
County Durham

British Library Cataloguing in
Publication Data.
A catalogue record for this book
is available from the
British Library

ISBN: 1-84104-066-5

Typeset by TW Typesetting, Plymouth, Devon
Printed by CPI, Bath

To Una

Contents

List of Illustrations

Foreword

By Sir Anthony O'Reilly OA, KBE
August 2006

There is a romantic story in Irish history about the battle at Ballyneety in 1690, prior to the siege of Limerick. A heavily guarded British military convoy was advancing toward the city of Limerick; the convoy decamped for the night and pickets were posted. The password was the name of the leader of the Irish forces, Patrick Sarsfeld, later Earl of Lucan. On that night Sarsfield led his troops through the darkness and when challenged by the enemy, 'Who goes there?' replied, 'Sarsfield is the word and Sarsfield is the man,' and battle was thus engaged.

The parallel in this is that Derek Finlay is the writer and Derek Finlay is the man. It runs right through the book, his clear sense of recollection, his authenticity, his sense of duty and honour, his sense of probity, and having worked with him for over 25 years, most important of all, his wisdom and sense of collegiality.

The book captures time and place in a manner which positions a Britain in transition. From the imperial grandeur of the nineteenth century, it was plunged into World War I where his father fought and he lost an uncle, and World War II, which so changed the universe.

Born in 1932, he was old enough to experience the Blitz of 1941 in London and, as is the manner of children, strangely to enjoy it, and importantly, to share in the fortitude of the British people as they stood alone against the world in 1940. Having left school in 1950, his 'gap' years of the early '50s were filled in a very meaningful way by national service. Derek enjoyed his national service, and particularly the experiences he underwent, and the people and the sights and sounds he became familiar with in Malaya and Singapore in 1950–52, and his participation in General Templer's ultimately successful campaign against the communist insurgency with his service as an officer in the Gordon Highlanders.

Having already been accepted by Emmanuel College in Cambridge – the 'other place' in Oxford folklore – he first arrived in

1952, initially to study economics and finally to study law, in which he did well, and graduated in 1955. But the preoccupation of his life then was rowing, something at which he was extremely good and which, in later years, he rekindled in the city of Pittsburgh where they have actually named a racing shell after him.

Another great love, one shared with me, was of Gilbert and Sullivan, and the thought of him performing 'The Three Little Maids' in the *Mikado* always crossed my mind when I later saw him make stern presentations on behalf of McKinsey or Heinz to groups of grim-faced businessmen.

He loved Cambridge and Cambridge loved him, and it was one of the defining periods of his career. It also enabled him to enjoy the love of his life, Una Grant, whom he had met in 1948 at 'dancing classes', no less, in his school. They decided to get engaged in 1955 and held their engagement party in Chapman's Garden at Emmanuel College, At their wedding they received many telegrams and congratulations including one from the Emmanuel Boat Club which was '10 to take her home', the coxswain's call to his crew towards the last yards of a winning race and the obvious title of this most excellent book. He married Una in 1956. They have proved an inspiration to each other, and this book celebrates it.

Despite meeting his future wife in 1948, the year was a tragic one for Derek, and he records it with sensitivity and an acknowledgement that, in the words of William Butler Yeats, 'all is changed – changed utterly' because in a period of four weeks, his beloved and admired brother Douglas, a wartime hero, winner of the DFC and an inmate of the infamous Stalag Luft III prison camp, was killed in an air crash, and his mother died. So at 16 years of age, he and his father were left, the last two remaining male members of the Finlay clan, another brother having died at age five from pneumonia.

Graduating in 1955 he joined Mobil Oil, then named *Socony Vacuum*, as a trainee and literally got his hands dirty learning about the interstices of the oil and refining business, but his great opportunity came in 1961 when he joined McKinsey – then a nascent consultant business in Great Britain – later to become a verb to describe good management. He acknowledges particularly the influence of Hugh Parker and Marvin Bower in raising management consultancy to a new level of professionalism and Socratic enquiry that brought great benefits to British and American business. It also brought him into contact with Heinz in a manner which ensured that in 1968 our paths would cross. After a stint in Chicago in 1965, he was elected a Principal of McKinsey in 1967, at a point in history when the McKinsey star was very much in the ascendant.

He tells some amusing stories about his early days as a McKinsey consultant with Tesco – now the giant of UK retailing. Then a company very much under control of its founder Sir Jack Cohen, Jack gave him a tie clip which was his private insignia and which within Tesco amounted almost to knighthood. It said, simply and unintelligibly, 'YCDBSOYA', which translates to 'you can't do business sitting on your ass', which has proved such a potent driving force for this great retailer ever since.

When I joined Heinz in 1969 I asked him and Carl Hoffman of the USA to help us reshape the UK company in a rapidly changing retail scene. It was to be the start of a long and very fruitful relationship. The book describes his early consulting work for Heinz and finally the acceptance of my invitation to join the Heinz Company in 1979 as Managing Director of what was then our largest overseas affiliate, and a major source of profit to the company, Heinz UK.

He, against an atmosphere of rapid change in British trading, the consolidation of multiples, the demise of the small retail outlet and the combativeness of the trade unions, provided a vital link to the adjustment overtaking Heinz UK. He came to the US in 1981 and joined the board of the Heinz Company. For the next twelve years we had adjoining rooms and enjoyed a period of unparalleled growth in the history of the company, which took it from a company that was worth less than $1 billion in May 1979 to one worth over $12 billion in 1993.

The book is hugely instructive on the methods of management that were used to achieve these goals and describes the immense amount of talent, thought and travel by many people that went into their achievement. He himself had the extremely important role of Senior Vice President of Corporate Development and, *inter alia*, of opening new worlds for the Heinz company. I remember his observation at one particular Corporate meeting, 'that 85 per cent of the New World had never heard of the Heinz name'. He travelled over 300,000 miles per year for twelve years and helped open markets in China, Thailand, India, Russia, South Korea and New Zealand for our company. He modestly says that when he left he had assisted in transforming Heinz into the most profitable US owned pure food company, emerging as a world wide global player in the world food industry. A clear case of British understatement.

Any student of rapidly evolving business practices will find his clear and concise analysis of the changing business scene hugely instructive. Nor does the book neglect the contrasts of the UK and the USA in terms of the working environment and the sociological force that made America the richest country in the world. His diagnosis of the difference between European health services and the more *laissez faire* but community driven system of US medical care is extremely thoughtful. His belief is that volunteerism in the USA is in stark contrast with the all pervasive sense of welfare state entitlement in much of Europe.

His recollections and experiences in Dawson International allow him to conclude that failure is as instructive as success, and his analysis of what the future holds for manufacturing businesses in the UK against the lower cost manufacturing base in the East is both incontestable and holds many ominous lessons ahead for European industry.

A thread runs through this book. It is about service. It is about duty. It is about standing by your mates. It is about doing the right thing. The inspiration for such spirit comes from many sources, but one of them must have been his affection for and respect of his father's war-time experiences in World War I.

His father fought in the Campaign of General Allenby of Arabia in World War I with his brother. In 1918 he had the agonising task of writing to an aunt asking her to console his mother at the death of his brother by sniper fire in a Turkish ambush.

That scene made an indelible impression upon Derek Finlay. It inspired his own pride in his work with the Gordon Highlanders in Malaya in 1950–52, and it is the obvious reinforcement to many of the actions that he took through his own life.

In Steven Spielberg's haunting film, *Saving Private Ryan*, the hero was eventually rescued by a platoon led by Captain John Miller. In rescuing him, the Captain was killed. Many years later, Private Ryan went back to the American Cemetery at Omaha Beach and knelt in front of the grave of the Captain, and in an emotionally-charged phrase said, 'Tell me I'm a good man.'

Anyone who reads this book will be able to answer this question and say that in the quality of his life, the objectives he has striven for, the sense of family he brings to all he does, the collegiality he shared with all his colleagues of which I am proud to number myself, Derek Finlay is 'a good man, and a fine companion'.

Sir Anthony O'Reilly OA, KBE

CHAPTER 1

My Early Years

I N HIS LATER YEARS MY FATHER always said to me that his generation had experienced more changes in the world around them than any previous generation or possibly any one generation following.

In 1890, the year in which William Templeton Finlay was born, there were no motorcars – nearly all traffic was horse drawn. There were no telephones, no television, no aeroplanes, and no modern drugs to combat life-threatening diseases. His father – also William, my grandfather – would occasionally drive my father in his horse-drawn trap from Putney to Esher for a 'special' outing!

My maternal grandfather, Thomas Jefferies, had his own practice as a dentist in Fulham – a profession that has also been transformed dramatically in the last half of the twentieth century and the early years of the twenty-first. Two of his sons carried on the tradition of dentistry, one taking over Grandfather's practice during World War I and the other starting his own practice in Kent on return from service in World War I in the East Surrey Regiment.

So in my time – a life spanning over two thirds of the twentieth century and seeing in the dawn of the new millennium – technology has in turn transformed my world. Instant communication, globalisation in business, economics and politics, the demise of the Cold War and the defeat of communism, and now, tragically, the curse of global terrorism – the challenge for the younger generation to fight to protect our freedom and civilised values in a society that has seen dramatic change in its lifestyles and standard of living. By present day definitions of poverty I spent a significant portion of my early years in that state!

It is against this background that I have a story to tell of a life of ambitions nurtured and shaped, many achieved, some frustrated and left by the wayside, financial independence well beyond my original hopes – all built on the bedrock of a wonderful wife and equally tolerant and supportive children.

My life began in May 1932 in the family home close to the Botanical Gardens at Kew near London. A warm-hearted and kind

The Jefferies family c. 1900. My maternal grandparents, aunts and uncles

woman, Phyllis, my mother, was third from youngest in a typical Victorian family of eleven children – over eighteen years separated her from the eldest child. My sympathies still go out to my grandmother when I think of the reality of giving birth to and nurturing such a large family! Inspired by their musical mother nearly every member of that family was a competent musician. Among them were a professional opera singer, violinists and several pianists including my mother. So perhaps it comes as no surprise that music and the enjoyment of it has played a large part in my life – but more of this family and its influence on me later.

My father was one of seven children – four sons and three daughters. An outstanding student aided by scholarships from the age of 11, at aged 16 he had reached Stage 5 in Mathematics and by 17 he had also completed a three-year course in Mechanical and Electrical Engineering and been awarded a First Class Diploma in the BSc course at South Western Engineering College under a Professor Pullen. In the following year with a further one-year scholarship, he worked on research on lubricants under the Professor. The results of that work were published by the Institution of Mechanical Engineers in May 1909.

A warm-hearted man, but strict in his ways and views on life, he believed that loyalty to and pride in one's country and the notion of giving service to the community and being a 'good citizen' were basic values: values that he cherished and strove to impart to his sons.

When I arrived in 1932 I had two brothers – Douglas who was nine years my senior, and Kenneth who was five years ahead of me. When I was nine months into my life tragedy struck the family. Brother Kenneth succumbed to double pneumonia and died – sadly before the coming of sulphonamide drugs and antibiotics, which surely would have enhanced the chances of saving his young life. Although I obviously never knew him I still treasure the picture of the impish looking red-headed brother I never had. At the same time I came close to death. Needless to say my parents' world collapsed, but I believe they sought solace in their religious faith. As Baptist and Church of England respectively, they felt let down and searched for 'answers' elsewhere. It was shortly thereafter that Christian Science entered into the family's beliefs and became the discipline under which Douglas and I were raised. Sunday morning service, Sunday School and Wednesday evening services were the order of the day through to our teen years until further tragedy overwhelmed my family later.

By the standards of the times we were comfortably – but not well – off. My father, or 'The Guv'nor' or 'Pop' as Douglas and I irreverently but affectionately called him, was well-established as the manager of a factory producing electrical products for telecommunications – telephones, both civil and military – and consumer electrical items such as electric irons and vacuum cleaners. Douglas was doing well at Richmond Hill School.

William Templeton Finlay – my father aged 65 in Kew Gardens

At aged five I was sent to a private preparatory school nearby within walking distance. There was no car in the family then although the Guv'nor had owned briefly some years earlier a bull-nosed twin-seater Morris with dickie seat in the rear which had moved on long before my arrival in the family.

It was also the start of my music tuition. I now realise the debt of gratitude I owe to my mother for her wisdom in how she introduced me to the piano. She was a very able pianist who, as the youngest but two in a very large and musical Victorian family, had been surrounded by music in various forms all her early life. Consequently, I too was aware of her piano playing as part of my earliest recollections. Her wisest move was in sending me to a private teacher who lived near our home and thus my musical tuition was kept separate from my formal schooling (apart from singing lessons). She never pressed me to take music lessons so my learning was at my pace and, even after allowing for the discipline of weekly piano lessons and practice, I carried on because I wanted to continue to learn and

Phyllis Finlay (née Jefferies) – my mother aged 22

explore the world of piano. In my early teens with my second private teacher, I discovered the wonderful music of the romantic composers: Chopin, Schumann, Brahms, Liszt and Mendelssohn. Privately I thought how wonderful it would be to become a concert pianist, until reality overtook my imaginings. I well remember pressing my music teacher to let me work on Chopin polonaises, ballades and scherzos – which she did, with some reluctance, at the cost of time she would have preferred me to spend practising Bach, Haydn, Mozart and others. At eighteen my lessons ceased when I started my National Service, but thirteen years of tuition left me able to 'go it alone' with reasonable confidence.

I know that if piano had been part of my formal education I would have probably given up. I did not warm to the master concerned or to his methods. So playing the piano has become both a hobby and a means of relaxation and a way to unwind. To do so required a piano so, until we could afford our own upright model, I would seek out nearby practice rooms to keep up whatever limited ability I had acquired. Now I am able to indulge in a superb Bluthner grand piano. A joy now is to hear Sarah, my eldest granddaughter, play and know that she too, if she so wishes, will always have this other world at her fingertips.

The headmistress of Kew College, Mrs Upton, had taught my brother before me. Fortunately or otherwise for me he had done rather well and had become one of the apples in her eye as far as she was concerned. This meant that I was never unaware for long of the academic challenge facing me between the ages of 5 and 10 as I was reminded of how well Douglas had done in this or that subject. The school uniform consisted of dark blue blazer, matching cap and grey short trousers, all of which quickly attracted the attentions – not always complimentary – of the local elementary school, as state primary schools were then called.

The grounding in the three Rs and French that I received at Kew College stood me in excellent stead when I moved on to my next school. I still recall with relish my introduction to the mysteries of algebra at the age of eight or nine. We were taught by a much younger lady teacher who was much more memorable than her subject. In the war years, silk stockings were unavailable and some ladies painted their legs a colour to represent the scarce stockings. Miss Hogan was such a lady! Such were the things that caught the attention of a young boy and, incidentally, are still remembered by the 74-year-old that he has since become.

One of the special boyhood 'treats' at that time was a visit with my parents to my Great-uncle Layton. Brother to my paternal grand-mother, Layton Crisp ran an impressive Victorian house in Chelsea in London. The front door was always opened by Willis, his butler, usually clad in green baize apron. We were then taken in to meet Uncle. Tea and often a game of bagatelle and then time for goodbye came. I was always hopeful that Uncle would squeeze a crisp white £5 note into my hand. He had set the precedent with Douglas and happily I was often spoiled in the same way! I try to remember Great-uncle Layton and his generosity when I see my own grandchildren now.

By 1938 war clouds were gathering and it was becoming obvious that Neville Chamberlain's piece of paper, waved on his arrival at Croydon after his Munich meeting with Adolf Hitler in 1937, was not worth the paper on which it was written along with his claim of

'Peace in our time'. The last resort of the appeasers was bound to fail against the unbridled and ruthless ambition of Hitler and his Nazi followers, lessons that should never, never, be forgotten by future generations.

By then Richmond Hill School, attended by Douglas, had gone out of business and he had been accepted at Emanuel School at Wandsworth. He rose to become School Captain, joined the OTC and was a passing good Earl of Warwick in a school production of Shaw's *Saint Joan*. My mother was very proud! In 1938 Emanuel School 'evacuated' itself to Petersfield to join up with Churcher's College. Douglas was billeted with a local family within cycling distance of the College and had soon joined the Local Defence Volunteers – or LDV – the forerunner of Dad's Army, better known as the Home Guard.

I suppose as the result of understandable concern for my safety, my parents decided that I too should be removed from harm's way. So my father – by then leader of the local ARP Wardens – was left alone at our home while Mother and I moved to a family friend's farm near Ross-on-Wye. A place was found for me at Ross High School some three miles from the farm. Mother walked me to school in the morning and was there to meet me at the end of the day to walk the three miles home – six miles a day for me and twelve miles for her: a far cry from the car-driven young and school-runs in 4 × 4s today. I really do believe we were the better for the exercise – both mother and son.

My time at the farm was a real eye-opener and learning experience. Riding on horse-drawn hay waggons, helping to bring in the harvest, wielding a pitchfork, being allowed to drive the one tractor on the farm and, best of all, sharing with the farm labourers their refreshments at break times – large wedge sandwiches filled with equally large wedges of cheese or beef washed down with gulps of cider.

This was the time of the 'phoney war' and after four or five months of relative calm in London, my parents decided that Mother and I should return home to Kew. As always, Murphy's Law came into play. No sooner had we returned home than the Blitz got under way with a vengeance. Looking back on this time I am amazed at the courage and fortitude that adults like my parents displayed when faced night after night and day after day with air-raids heralded by the undulating wail of the sirens, followed by the drone of German bombers, the continuous anti-aircraft gunfire, and the sequential crumps as sticks of bombs – usually in threes or fives – detonated as they hit the ground. Collecting and trading pieces of shrapnel – some still warm – found in the streets became the 'in thing' at school; much more fashionable than playing conkers (now for some absurd politically-correct reason banned in today's schools – presumably because of a risk of damage to the wee lad or lass and the consequent risk of a teacher or school being sued by aggrieved parents – oh dear!).

For the duration of the war we lived with a half-complete Anderson shelter in our garden – or at least the half dug-out hole for it! I assume that my father decided that the basement cellar would be more commodious and offer better protection than corrugated iron. So the cellar was duly cleared, cleaned and whitewashed and wooden bunks built. The most memorable of the many nights spent there was the night of the massive German incendiary bomb raid on London when St Paul's stood out in the night sky silhouetted against the fleeting shafts of light from the searchlights and the smoke and flames of London burning.

Incendiary bombs fell everywhere and Mother and I were awakened in the middle of that night by the stench of smoke emanating from an incendiary bomb that had exploded beside the cellar air vent. Its magnesium contents were fizzing away and pouring acrid smoke into the cellar. As Chief Warden, my father had ensured that the mandatory buckets of sand and water plus a coiled stirrup pump were sitting on our front porch ready for action if needed. One of his team of wardens was passing our house on patrol, saw the fire and dashed to douse the incendiary bomb – unfortunately with water – which action only encouraged the bomb to burn more fiercely. By this time my father had arrived. Not known normally for his use of strong language, events got the better of him and he issued immediate instructions: 'Put bloody sand on it – not water!' – or words to that effect!

Some time after that 'event', early one morning after a night-long air-raid, my father's eldest brother Peter, his wife Ada and my two cousins, Joan and Nancy, arrived out of the blue with their dog. During the night a land mine had come to rest on the railway bridge near their home in Sheen and the police had evacuated everyone within the potential danger-zone while the bomb disposal squad got to work to defuse it. We all waited anxiously, wondering whether it would detonate or be made safe. We had lunch together; still no news either way. Then around 2.30 p.m. there was an enormous crump – the mine had detonated! Our windows shook but did not break – our house was about 2½ miles away from the railway bridge. Miraculously the bomb squad was safe. Anticipating that the mine was becoming unsafe they had run for their lives. One had nearly all his clothes blown off and his colleague lost his hearing. Equally miraculously most of the blast must have gone upwards rather than outwards. Consequently the damage to my cousins' home was relatively minor – but they went home expecting the worst. Such was the 'luck of the draw' during those times – agonising for adults, almost part of the fun of growing up for children, providing never to be forgotten memories in later life.

In the summer of 1942 my parents decided that my prep schooldays were over and that I should move on. For some reason there was never a thought of following in my brother's footsteps to Emanuel School. Perhaps they were concerned at sending me off to Petersfield where Emanuel was still located. So after visits and interviews at several schools I was accepted at Kingston Grammar School at Kingston-upon-Thames in Surrey. Then it was a Direct Grant maintained school of some 380 pupils with a good academic and sporting record. Today it is nearly double in size, independent, co-educational and achieving academic results far in excess of those achieved in my day. Placed in Middle-Three in September 1942, I was moved up to Upper-Three at half-term and thereafter spent eight very happy years moving up through the upper stream in each academic year.

Fees were £12 per term. In my third year I was awarded an Exhibition Scholarship, which reduced my fees still further. At 15, I sat the Oxford & Cambridge School Certificate Examination and managed to achieve eight credits. I then moved into the Sixth Form (Arts and Classics) and two years later secured passes in English, History and Latin in the London University Higher School Certificate Examination. I was awarded a County Major Scholarship in 1949 and my ambition then shifted to the possibility of following my brother up to Emmanuel College, Cambridge where he had gone in 1941.

But before my story moves on I must go back to 1945 – the year the war in Europe ended. With the German surrender on Lüneburg

Heath came the prospect of freedom for my brother and his safe return home.

In 1940 he had gone up to Emmanuel College at Cambridge University to read Engineering after leaving Emanuel School where he had done well, becoming Captain of School and a member of the school shooting team. At Emmanuel he joined the University Air Squadron. In 1941 his stay at Emmanuel was interrupted when he was called up and enlisted in the Royal Air Force Volunteer Reserve (RAFVR) with the rank of Leading Aircraftman and, shortly thereafter, Acting Pilot Officer. He volunteered for aircrew and was shipped out to New Brunswick, Canada to begin his flight training. I believe that, as part of the anxiety of the US Government not to be seen to be too open in its assistance to the UK, his stay in Canada was short and he was then sent to Florida, USA, to start serious training at No. 5 Flying Training School at Clewiston where he earned his 'Wings'.

Shipped back to the UK on the liner *Queen Elizabeth*, by then in its grey wartime colours, he completed his training on bombers and was posted to 103 Squadron, Bomber Command, based at Elsham Wolds in Lincolnshire, as a bomber pilot flying a Lancaster bomber. In addition to himself, his seven-man crew consisted of one Canadian, one Australian, one Cornishman, and three other Brits. They completed 25 bombing raids – 'Ops' – against targets in the Ruhr, Berlin and Milan. On the night of 24 September 1943 during their 26th Op over Mannheim, Germany, they were shot down by a Messerschmitt 109 fighter. All managed to leave the stricken aircraft. Douglas was the last to bale out, by which time the engines were on fire, and he had managed to hold the plane on a level course.

Back at home our first inkling of anything untoward was a telegram from the Air Ministry informing my parents that Douglas was 'missing on operations', giving no indication as to whether he and his crew were dead or alive, or taken prisoner.

Some six weeks later the morning post was delivered. Suddenly my mother shrieked aloud, 'Doug is safe!' A German postcard from him told us he was safe, unhurt and a POW in Stalag Luft III – the high security camp where Germany imprisoned captured Allied aircrew officers. So started an irregular correspondence with my brother using a simple system of numbering letters and cards to check that none went missing.

Douglas William Finlay with his bomber crew, 103 Squadron, Bomber Command, Elsham Wolds, Lincs, 1943 – my eldest brother

By early 1945 it was becoming clear that the end of the war in Europe was in sight and that Germany's total defeat was inevitable. On 3 May 1945 we received a telegram from Douglas to say that he had been liberated at Lübeck and expected to be home in a few days. He also penned a note on 2 May from RAF Trenthorst:

Dears,
    The great moment came at 1 o'clock today when an armoured car with a real-live Tommy perched on it came rolling up. Boy oh Boy! What a sight. I've no idea how long it will take to get home but I guess 14 days should do it.
    My love to everyone
    God bless, see you soon. Doug

Six days later, on 8 May, our family was at home celebrating VE Day. With us were my Uncle Peter, my father's eldest brother, his wife and my cousins. Just after lunch, one of us noticed the front gate open. A knock on the front door, opened by one of us, and standing there in a new RAF blue battledress was my brother – a moment I shall never forget as long as I live. I remember him drinking two pints of milk straight off and the still drawn face on him that reflected his own exhilaration at finally being free again – really the whole issue the war had been about for all of us.

Douglas had been awarded the DFC while still a POW. Soon after his homecoming he attended an investiture at Buckingham Palace to receive his decoration from the King. Only two guests were allowed to accompany him and be present. Needless to say Father and Mother went with much excitement and I got the short straw to await them outside the Palace.

One year later he was formally demobilised. So in October 1946 he returned to Emmanuel College to resume his degree studies reading Economics, having switched from Engineering.

At the time of his homecoming, I had no inkling of what he and hundreds of others of Allied POWs had undergone at the hands of their German captors prior to their liberation. After his death, when my father and I had his papers, I had noted in his POW log/diary a reference to 'The Great Trek' which had started on 24 January 1945 at one hour's notice when his hut had been told to pack up and be ready to leave their camp as the Russian forces were getting near. His POW log records the incredibly tough conditions that he and his fellow prisoners were forced to undergo in appalling weather – temperatures 40 degrees below, inadequate clothing, and little or no overnight shelter as they were force-marched for days covering up to 40 kilometres per day. Here is an extract:

'The Great Trek'

Verbatim extract from the wartime POW log of Flight Lieutenant D.W. Finlay, DFC, Room 6, Block 123, North Compound, Stalag Luft III, Sagan, Germany

January 27 1945: This afternoon there is tremendous excitement again in the Camp when the OKW states that the Russians have extended their bridgehead across the Oder at Steinau and are fighting north of this point. Is freedom at hand or will the Germans move us before the Russian Armies can reach Sagan? In the evening Polly brings us rumours of Kriegies marching 150 kilos in 6 days in appalling weather. We poo-poo these but are all secretly rather worried. At 8.30 we have had supper and I am making toffee when 'Fagan' is told to stand by tonight for bigger work. He, Mike and I are discussing when and if the Russians will reach here when Deacon rushes in with news, 'Pack your things, we're off in an hour'!! And so our trek began . . .

Sat. 27.1.45: Packed and ate all we could, destroyed all clothing, cigarettes and food left: sat up waiting to move. Mild night, plenty of snow.

Sun. 28.1.45: Finally moved off 0400 hrs — collected food parcel each and set off on Gorlitz road. Halbau at 0830 and Friewaldau at 1400 — civilians quite friendly — marched on at 15.30 reaching Springruh at dusk — bitterly cold. Paddy all in — Curly and I carry him — long walt fur a barn — 12 hrs rest. Distance 35 kilos — worst day of all.

Mon. 29.1.45: Arose at 0700 and moved off at 0800, bought sledge for packet of prunes — bitterly cold and snowing — left Gorlitz Road after 2–3 kilos and turned NW — Prilbus at noon. Past Russian prison camp 1400. Paddy, Mike, Deacon and Johnny in bad way — Muskau at 1900 — quartered in Theatre — crowded but warm and dry — hot brew and a good wash — distance 30 kilos.

Tues. 30.1.45: Quiet day at Muskau — people friendly trading for cigs etc. Germans supply bread and marg at last.

Wed. 31.1.45: Another day at Muskau — Yanks left at noon for Nürnberg — bartering with children in evening.

Thurs. 1.2.45: Dep. postponed — thawing rapidly — talk to survivors of Herman Goering Panzer unit from Litmanstadt, ordered to move at 1700 — departed with sledges at 2300.

Fri. 2.2.45: Sledges abandoned after 4 km — packed up! — heavy going carrying food — reached Granstun at dawn, 3 hrs sleep in a barn. 0730–1030 — marched on to Spremberg — reached Military Barracks at 1400 hrs — Germans supply hot meal — joined by East Camp — left 1400 hrs on train 1730. Distance for day 30 km — 40 officers/cattle truck — departed about midnight.

Sat. 3.2.45: Hohenbock at 0830, Ruhland 1030 and Plessa 1120 — crossed Elbe 1520 at Jorgau — Halle 2030 hrs — long waits, but generally quick travel — hardly room to lie down at night.

Sun. 4.2.45: Hildeshum 0700 — fine and worried about air attacks on train — Hanover at 0800 — some bomb damage. Verden 1200–1500 — first water of trip — atrocious treatment — Tarmstadt at 1630 — left train and marched 3 km to Marlag — reach camp 1730, kept waiting in wet until midnight while 2000 POW were searched — finally in bed about 0100 hrs and so to sleep.

Transcribed by his brother, R.D. Finlay, 22.4.03.

But I and many others of my generation had little idea at the time of the real horrors of that Trek and its cost in intense hardship and loss of life among the POWs involved, until the recent publication of *The Last Escape* written by Paul Brickhill. The march went on for just over three months and covered nearly 450 miles north-east from Stalag Luft III in Silesia towards Berlin and northern Germany under quite appalling conditions. Stalag Luft III was only one of virtually all the Allied POW camps that were force-marched westwards away from the advancing Russian forces. The Germans' purpose appears to have been the possibility of using Allied POWs as bargaining chips in securing better terms from the Allies when surrender became inevitable or in fear of Allied reprisals should the Germans either carry out mass executions of prisoners or let them fall into Russian hands.

In January 2003 I had a call from cousin Joan who had been at my home with her family when Douglas arrived home unexpectedly on VE Day in 1945. She wanted to know whether I had heard of the book. She had been given a copy and had realised as she read it what my brother must have undergone with so many others literally days before he arrived home in 1945.

So I bought a copy immediately and as I read it, and in particular the chapter covering the exit from Stalag Luft III, I realised I was reading virtually the continuation of my brother's log. Even more uncanny was to see confirmation of other parts of Douglas's log entries – the map of his compound, the location of his hut which turned out to be the location of one of the three tunnels portrayed in the film *The Great Escape*, and the identical drawing of the camp layout.

To return again to my story. I enjoyed my schooldays at Kingston. Academically I held my own – aptly described by 'Jimmy James', my headmaster, in a reference he prepared for me before his retirement in 1949:

> I have known him since September 1942, and have watched his development with interest and appreciation. He has always been in the upper of three parallel streams and has held a good place therein, averaging 8th out of 32 throughout.

In those days you could indulge your athletic skills in several sports, unlike the regime today, which requires specialisation to be able to reach standards necessary for successful competition. So I was fortunate to be selected for the School 1st Hockey XI for two seasons, playing alongside team-mates who went on to achieve national, international and Olympic honours – Don Wilson (Captain of Scotland and GB Olympic Squad), 'Dickie' Dale (Wales), Pat Austen (England) and Mike Doughty (England and Captain GB Olympic Squad), plus several County caps. I was asked to fill-in in an Anglo-Irish Trial. I enjoyed the game but unfortunately a thief rifled the changing rooms and I lost my wallet and watch – the latter more special to me than the money as it had been Douglas's.

On the athletic track I was a good sprinter (100 and 220 yards) and for several years held the school javelin record. For two years I was Captain of the sport. But my long-term sporting association was with rowing. I think three factors generated my interest. First my maternal grandfather had amassed a small collection of 'pots' rowing in Fours and Double Sculls for St James and Soho Rowing Club in 1885 and 1886. Second my brother was already into the sport rowing in Emanuel School's 1st VIII before he went up to Emmanuel College, Cambridge in 1940. He rowed there when he returned to complete his degree course after being demobbed in 1946. Finally, in 1945 only six to eight boys at Kingston had any serious interest in rowing despite the school's pre-war accomplishments in the sport. So, Phil Dougall and I and several others started 'tubbing' and put together a clinker four using Kingston Rowing Club's boathouse as our base. By 1948 we had developed our skills to the point where we had an eight racing shell on the water, along with rum-tum single sculls, and were competing in local regattas. One day we returned from an outing and noticed that we were being watched by a gentleman in an open top Rolls-Royce wearing a soft grey fedora style hat with the brim turned down. He got out of the car, strode over and asked in a soft voice, 'Would you like some coaching help? I used to row here myself years ago.' From then on the Old Kingstonian, well-known author of *Journey's End* and playwright R.C. Sherriff, was increasingly generous of his time and support. He provided us with a new shell eight and was in fact a good coach.

He invited the 1st VIII to dinner at Scott's restaurant in the Strand and afterwards to see his new play in the West End – Ralph Richardson was taking the lead part. We were late arriving at the theatre and to our surprise the curtain had been held until we were seated. Never since have I enjoyed such privileged treatment! His name will always be remembered as the major benefactor of rowing at the school which as I write now numbers among the most successful in the UK.

Our other piece of good fortune was the arrival of a new master with rowing experience who was prepared to take over rowing. Harry Bygrave was a real enthusiast and provided the momentum that along with Sherriff's help got rowing seriously established as a leading sport at Kingston.

On a Thursday afternoon in mid July 1948, we had just finished a House Fours Competition. I returned home to be met by Douglas who by then had achieved his degree and come down from Emmanuel. He told me that our mother had been taken ill suddenly. Several days later she died from a myocardial infarction – coronary thrombosis. My parents had put their faith in Christian Science, and at this time of crisis my father looked to his faith to bring my mother through this illness. The sad and tragic result was that his trust was misplaced. Without medical help she could not make it. So on 25 July her life ended prematurely at age 52 – a terrible waste and loss to her family.

Douglas had rejoined the Cambridge University Air Squadron on his return to Emmanuel in 1946 and to his great joy was up in the air again piloting Tiger Moths rather than Lancaster Bombers. Each year the Squadron held its two-week annual camp at Shoreham Flying Club on the Sussex coast – overlooked by Lancing College where Gordon Crisp, a cousin of my father, was School Medical Officer. Indeed in 1947 I had joined Douglas for a short stay in camp. There he took me up in the forward cockpit of a Tiger Moth for my first flight over the South Downs. The inter-com packed up shortly after take-off so I had no forewarning of steep climbs and loops – but nevertheless a fantastic feeling being for the first time 'detached' from terra firma!

Due to attend camp in late August 1948 at the same time as our normal family holiday Douglas suggested that, in view of Mother's death, he would miss camp and join Father and me on our previously arranged holiday at Herne Bay. Father insisted that life should go on as normal and that Douglas should go ahead with his camp. So Father and I went to Herne Bay and Douglas went to Shoreham.

So imagine my utter disbelief and horror when early in the second week, on 24 August, Father received news that Douglas and another ex RAF pilot from Selwyn College, Gus Forder, had been killed when their Tiger Moth did not come out of a practice dive over

Horsham and crashed into the garden of Hilaire Belloc, the writer and poet, and his daughter Mrs Jebb. So in just four weeks I had lost my mother and brother and my father had lost his wife and eldest son. A second family funeral followed attended by stunned and disbelieving relatives just four weeks after my mother's funeral. Uniformed fellow officers bore his coffin draped in the Union Flag. In the ensuing days and weeks I found it almost impossible to maintain my composure. I just could not talk to friends or relatives offering sympathy without a trembling lip and tears welling up in my eyes.

My father's loss must have been too terrible to bear. He stayed in mourning for a year, but insisted life should carry on as normal as possible. It was during that period that I learned how to handle cooking and limited tailoring! My loss was different. In the time since he returned home after his liberation from Stalag Luft III in June 1945, Douglas and I had started to get to know each other. Our nine-year age gap seemed to be closing. He was virtually engaged to a super WAAF girl – Dorothy, or Dot as we knew her – who had served with him in 103 Squadron at Elsham Wolds, the Bomber Command airfield in Lincolnshire from whence he had flown his 26 sorties before being shot down by an ME 109 in September 1943 over Mannheim, Germany and taken prisoner. He had lined up his first job in the Transport Department of Smith's Industries and the future looked promising. To this day I wonder how my and my family's lives would have been affected had he lived – ours not to reason why.

Towards the end of August Father decided we should take a break after the anguish of recent weeks. We boarded the Flying Scotsman bound for Edinburgh to sample the second year of the new Edinburgh Festival. We stayed at the North British Hotel – now the Balmoral. The highlight for me of this visit was to attend a performance of Beethoven's seventh symphony in the Usher Hall. Played by the Philharmonia Orchestra, conducted by Rafael Kubelik, it was memorable – in particular the delicacy of the Allegretto movement followed by the resounding vigour of the final movement. We also spent time in Fife trying, unsuccessfully, to trace earlier family contacts there.

In September 1948 I was appointed Captain of School at Kingston – a pity that neither mother nor Doug was there to know; I think they would have been as proud as my father was. Responsibilities at school provided needed therapy for me and helped restore my composure. One avant-garde development at that time was the introduction of dancing classes to help us boys develop some social graces. Invitations to sixth formers used to arrive via the Head's office from neighbouring girls' schools to their dances (interesting that boys' schools never seemed to hold school dances!). I remember on one occasion I managed to miss the last bus home. So after a six-mile walk home I arrived on the doorstep, and knocked on the front door. It was opened by Douglas, with a rather impish grin on his face: 'The Guv'nor wants to see you!' he said ominously. A not unreasonable ticking-off ensued and the lesson was learned.

In autumn 1948 a formal agreement was reached between our school and Surbiton High School. A select number of senior boys would attend Surbiton's dancing classes. So along we went and started to tackle the intricacies of the tango, foxtrot, quickstep, waltz, etc. Among the bevy of attractive girls who were present at these classes was an especially attractive girl. She had shortish dark hair and a winning smile and seemed full of life. Her name was Una Grant. She was to become my wife nine years later.

So at age 17, with my father's strong support, I found myself with a third year in the sixth form readying myself to sit Emmanuel

Una

College's Previous Examination in November 1949, after passing Higher School Certificate in July of that year. I arrived at Cambridge by train and was lodged for two nights in digs in Warkworth Street and had my first experience of a Cambridge landlady. The exam, along with the admission interview with the College Fellows, took two days. Also in the same digs was another would-be Emmanuel entrant from St Peter's School, York. Barry Mortimer was to become a lifelong friend and fellow undergraduate and to build a distinguished legal career, latterly as a Judge in Hong Kong. On Thursday evening after the first day's exams I decided to walk across Parker's Piece and find my way to King's College Chapel to hear Evensong – a never to be forgotten experience in the candlelit beauty of that place. The choir was wonderful – a foretaste of the special opportunities to come as an undergraduate in that University.

I managed to pass the exam and perform reasonably coherently during the interview with College Fellows and my session with the Master, Edward Welbourne – of whom more later. So in December 1949, Father and I received the news that I had been accepted and should take up my place in October 1952, after completion of my National Service.

So started the next phase in my life. I had left school at age 18 in summer 1950. I had a very attractive girlfriend with whom I found a great deal in common and had formed a strong attachment and whose parents offered me exceptional hospitality and friendship.

Chapter 2

National Service and Matters Military

I N 1915 MY FATHER AND HIS younger brother Douglas enlisted
together in the 2nd Battalion of the 14th London Regiment, better
known then and today as the London Scottish. They were together
in the Machine Gun Platoon and were very close. Together they
served in Salonika and Palestine. In late April 1918 they were
involved in fierce fighting against Turkish opposition in the desert on
the road to Es Salt in the hills of Moab near the river Jordan. Douglas
came under severe fire and was killed by sniper fire while binding up
a wounded London Scot.

When clearing up my father's papers after his death in 1973, I came
upon a letter that he had written to an aunt several days after his
brother's death on 1 May 1918 to tell her of his death. I quote it
below in its entirety. Its poignancy needs no comment from me.

JAMES DOUGLAS FINLAY

*Copy of a letter written by my father, William Templeton, his brother, to their
aunt and uncle (Crisp) on 11 May 1918 following Douglas' death in action
at Es Salt, Palestine, on 1 May 1918*

Saturday, May 11th

Dear Auntie and Uncle,

Perhaps you have already heard from home – in which case my
news will not prove quite such a shock, but in any case I just feel I
must write and tell you the sad news – tho' I would give anything not
to have to.

Dear Douglas – or as the boys all call him affectionately – 'Dougal'
– was killed in action on May 1st – and even now I cannot quite
realise it.

We have been so long together and come safely through so many
dangers, that I – in fact both of us – almost counted the days until we
should be back home again; and now he is taken and I have to plough
a lonely furrow – 'C'est la Guerre'.

We were attacking a strong Turkish position beyond the Jordan –
in the Hills of Moab – on the road to Es Salt – when our company
ran up against a tough job.

Most of us crossed safely through two or three wadis swept by machine gun and rifle fire, and then we had to cross a ridge; what lay beyond we could only conjecture, and when we actually did cross we found it was a wadi absolutely swept from all sides by machine guns and rifles.

Thank God – all had not to cross, and to my team fell the lot of covering the flank with my gun – else one wonders?

Doug got safely across and, with some wounded, took refuge in a cave, and here whilst binding these boys up, he was shot in the head and almost instantly killed – Just uttering – 'I'm hit' – and then he was gone – 'Great Laddie' –

We wondered how they fared; but it was such a death trap that it was some time before a messenger got through to us that were left.

At last one chap ran the gauntlet safely, and they later sent out to me to tell me about dear old Dougal.

We could do nothing until night fell – and so we had to wait through the long afternoon until under the cover of darkness our company could withdraw.

All I can say is that I hope it will never fall to anyone else's lot to endure hours such as I spent up in those hills – that afternoon.

Its memory will be with me forever – for Doug and I were like 'David and Jonathan' together – and now he is gone. It is a big price to pay.

In the dark I left my post for a few minutes Auntie – to make quite sure, – for I tried to tell myself it must be some mistake – and then I met them bringing him back.

So I and Douglas met for the last time alone – and I kissed him farewell for us all Auntie.

My thoughts and the agony of those few moments God alone knows.

Next day – away in the plains – we buried our boys – officers and men side by side – and in a quiet little God's acre just at dusk – near the Jordan. It was a glorious service – with both Presbyterian and C of E padres present – and to the sound of three volleys and a lament on the pipes we both loved – with its sad sorrowful yearning – we left them peacefully sleeping.

Almost I think I buried part of my heart there too with Dougal.

Now we are out resting in the hills for a day or two – and it all seems an awful dream – but I miss Douglas terribly.

Still triumphing over everything Auntie and greater than our grief is the noble way he died – 'Ministering to his boys' – and I cannot help but feel proud – very proud of him.

Everyone has been very kind in their sympathy and it is nice to know he was loved. Many are the tales of heroism I could tell you of that day – but it would take too long. Just one I must.

One boy – 'Coulie' – as we call him – lay near to Doug's sergeant who was mortally wounded also. 'Halley' – he said to the boy next to him 'I must go over and see if I can help Sgt Walker.' Halley tried to dissuade him for he knew Sgt Walker would not last – and it was death to move; but – he said 'Coulie' would not be gainsayed and the entreaty in his voice was a thing to marvel at.

Suddenly Coulie dashed across to the Sgt and as he bent over him – a shot killed him instantly – 'Greater love hath no man than to lay down his life for a friend'.

Glorious this Auntie – and it makes one feel proud to have had such comrades – Heroes every one of them that day.

So I pray that in the days to come we may prove somewhat worthy of the sacrifice these boys have made for us.

I saw Peter a day or two back in the plain and thank God he was safe and well.

But it is of dear little Mother I am thinking always. Away here we can do so little to soften the blow – except to pray that God will be good to her and Dad, and just make them brave in their sorrow. So we must wait until that day dawns when we shall all meet 'Across the Bourne'.

Auntie if you can manage it – pay Mother a visit – just to lift her a bit from her sorrow – and you'll be doing us boys a big favour.

I hope that all is well in your little home circle. Give my love to Uncle and yourself.

With fondest wishes,
Your loving Nephew,
Willie.

Transcribed from the original by R. Derek Finlay at Grantully Castle on 11 July 1999.

I have included the above in my story because it provides an understanding of my father's great affection for his old regiment that endured to the end of his days and did, I believe, have a significant influence on my military experiences.

When my time for National Service arrived the length of service had just been increased from 18 to 24 months. There was much comment about the waste of time it represented, interruption to one's career, further education and the like. I was determined to avoid it being a waste of time in my own case and to get something of value out of my service. I had been active in the School Cadet Corps as CSM, which maybe influenced my concerns. The London Scottish had been affiliated for many years with the Gordon Highlanders, a first-rate Highland Regiment. So with my agreement my father contacted the Colonel of the Gordons, Colonel William 'Willy' Graham, to seek his support for me to be accepted into the Gordons for my National Service. I knew he had succeeded when I received my call-up papers, travel warrant and instruction to report on 21 September 1950 to the Highland Brigade Training Centre at Fort George on the Moray Firth near Inverness. So began my long association with one of the finest infantry regiments in the British Army.

To the thousands of National Servicemen who did their basic training at the Fort and to local folk, Fort George is a very well known landmark. Constructed by General Wade as part of the London Government's 'pacification' of the Highlands after the Battle of Culloden in 1746 and the collapse of the Jacobite cause, it began service in the 1770s as an English garrison. One of the largest military fortifications in western Europe, it has never seen a shot fired in anger and is now, after a very expensive restoration, primarily a tourist attraction in the hands of Scottish National Heritage, although still with a modest army presence.

I can assure you that in 1950 it had changed little since the 1770s! For me it was a culture shock of significant proportions. After issue of kit I found myself in a small stone-floored barrack room with seven or eight fellow conscripts with backgrounds as diverse as their accents – from Manchester, the North-East, Glasgow etc. My vocabulary expanded exponentially! Ablution facilities were basic. An outside bathhouse and cold water only and any heat that there was vented mostly to the outdoors.

A severe 'boot camp' atmosphere prevailed. All Highland regimental badges were there – Seaforth, Black Watch, Cameron, Gordon, Argyll and even the odd HLI – both as 'Jocks' and as our instructors. Life immediately became a flurry of injections (double doses if you did not move along the line fast enough), drill parades with yelling and challenges to one's manhood that today would have human rights lawyers and other 'do-gooders' having a field day. Runs on the pebble beach with new hobnail boots gave a whole new meaning to 'running in'. After six weeks 'square bashing' I and several others in my squad were moved to a Junior Leader Platoon whose main benefit was to be moved from my cold barrack room in the Fort to a spider barrack room equipped with stoves and respectable washing facilities located over the drawbridge outside the Fort.

For the next few weeks as potential Officer and NCO candidates we were given more training in weaponry and fieldcraft and sent out on overnight exercises. Here I learned the value of a stone warmed in a campfire as a substitute hot water bottle in below freezing night temperatures. During this time I was selected to attend a War Office Selection Board (WOSB) in Barton Stacey in Hampshire. I made the grade and survived the subtle psychological tests and theoretical 'situations' placed before us such as how to get six soldiers across a theoretical 20-foot ravine with one wooden plank and a 16-foot length of rope!

I have vivid memories of life in that spider barrack room outside just over the wooden bridge entrance to the Fort. We were a motley mix of public and grammar school boys each wearing a different cap badge. In November we were suddenly issued with highland dress – Kilmarnock bonnet, regimental Jock kilt, white gaiters, diced hose, hair sporran and brogue shoes. We were to be the first National Service Guard of Honour at the ceremony of the Installation of the Governor of Edinburgh Castle and a Remembrance Service at St Giles' Cathedral.

We entrained at Inverness station en route for Edinburgh Waverley. At Perth, the rear half of the train was decoupled and carried on to Glasgow. Unfortunately Rory McEwen (to become a well known society cabaret artist and guitarist) found himself in the toilet in the Glasgow-bound section with his kit with the rest of us on our way to Edinburgh – he joined us later! We were billeted in Redford Cavalry Barracks and carried out our duties impeccably. I discovered that wearing a kilt on parade on the Castle Esplanade on a very windy and gusty day can leave a soldier's dignity very exposed with precious little that he can do about it. With only three days' leave over Christmas there was insufficient time to go home so I went to my uncle's sister at Cults near Aberdeen for Christmas Day and then straight back to Fort George on the next day – no celebration of Boxing Day in Scotland then.

In January 1951 I finally left Fort George and arrived at Eaton Hall Officer Cadet School as an Officer Cadet to start the 5-month course of instruction with a view to Passing Out with a King's Commission. Known as the St Pancras Station of the North-West because of its similarity to the London Station of that name (both designed by the same architect), it was a cavernous building with Nissen type barrack blocks in its grounds. I was assigned to 15 Platoon, C Company, which lived in one of the outside blocks. There I met men, a number of whom were to become lifelong friends, such as Paddy Gibbs who was commissioned into the Dorset Regiment and whose friendship I was to renew when I retired to Grantully, and Ian Petrie, commissioned into the Seaforth Highlanders. I met Ian again when he was a Senior Executive with United Biscuits and I was with McKinsey & Co doing a consulting assignment at his company; he now lives not far from Grantully. All three of us along with Mitch Mitchell, a fine chap from Shetland, then in the Army Education Corps, became Junior Under Officers under our Senior Under Officer Richard van Oss, an old Radleighan.

Much has been written elsewhere about the Hall and the hundreds of National Service Infantry Officers who received their commissions there to leave to join their regiments scattered at that time all over

Under Officers, C Company, Eaton Hall Officer Cadet School, April 1951. 'Mitch' Mitchell, John Capito, Paddy Gibbs, Ian Petrie, Richard van Oss (RDF took the picture)

the world. But one personal experience bears recounting. As I recall, on Tuesday and Thursday each week, a drill parade took place at 0600 hours under the direction of Regimental Sergeant Major Copp of the Coldstream Guards. Over 6 feet tall, he was an imposing figure resplendent in highly polished buttons and gleaming leather Sam Browne with drill stick at the ready.

On a particular Tuesday parade with all companies on the parade ground we were practising the 'Fix Bayonets' movement. Having got the bayonet secured on the boss of the rifle we received the order 'Slope Arms'. There was a clatter of steel hitting the ground further down the rank from me. A booming enquiry followed from RSM Copp: 'What's the matter with you, Sir?' Back came an unforgettable reply in a very fruity voice, 'Sorry Staff – I appear to have speared myself with my bayonet!' For a moment Copp was lost for words then, words to the effect: 'Well don't do it again!'

The following Thursday same parade, same drill movement, same clatter of bayonet and rifle hitting the ground from the same position down the rank from me. A similar enquiry from RSM Copp. And then the punchline reply: 'Sorry Staff – much the same trouble as last Tuesday!' At this, Copp could take no more: the hapless Officer Cadet must be removed to safety. 'Sergeant Pile, double him off to the Guard Room.'

Unlike its Regular army officer equivalent at the Royal Military Academy at Sandhurst, where the three-year curriculum and teaching focus was to produce the senior officers of the future skilled in the broad-based arts of war, Eaton Hall's job was to turn out Platoon Commanders who could take up such commands and acquit themselves competently in low level battle conditions if required. Thus I believe that an Eaton Hall trained second lieutenant was in many cases more able get to grips with the down to earth jobs of leading patrols in Malaya, fighting Mau Mau in East Africa or keeping hordes of Chinese attackers at bay in the Korean War and similar situations elsewhere than his more academically trained Regular equivalent. Of course there were many exceptions that disproved the rule but I believe I was right for the majority.

In May 1951 Passing Out Parade arrived and in the company of our relatives (Father was there) Charlie Company passed out in the presence of Princess Elizabeth and we were granted the King's Commission. I had achieved my goal and became Second Lieutenant

Finlay, The Gordon Highlanders – a proud moment for my father and me, and Una.

I was posted to the First Battalion recently arrived in Malaya from Germany and engaged on anti-terrorist operations as part of the Emergency – or war – then under way, trying to rid the country of communist guerillas bent on the overthrow of the Government and the expulsion of the British. After two weeks' embarkation leave I boarded HMT *Empire Pride*, a 9000-ton troopship, at Liverpool Docks. To the tune of 'Goodnight Irene', played by the band on the dockside, I and two thousand other servicemen set sail for my next adventure – active service in the Far East.

CHAPTER 3

On His Majesty's Active Service

I THOUGHT I HAD SEEN 'most of it' when I arrived in September 1950 at Fort George and underwent my basic training. However within two or three hours of embarking on the HMT *Empire Pride* – a 9,000-ton troopship – I was given my first command – as a Troop Deck Officer in charge of a deck full of 250 or so NCOs and servicemen. They were a motley lot, mostly National Servicemen on their way like me to Singapore or beyond to Hong Kong or on to Kure, Japan, to join the British forces fighting in the Korean War. Others were regular servicemen returning to their units after home leave.

Everything was going well until we reached the Bay of Biscay. It lived up to its stormy and sickening reputation until we rounded Cape St Vincent into the calmer waters offshore Portugal and sailed into Gibraltar. To the envy of many of us – still green from the effects of sea sickness! – one lucky soldier was put ashore with suspected appendicitis which meant he would probably be returned to the UK.

Next stop was Valetta harbour in Malta to refuel and then on to Port Said for about eight hours' shore leave before starting our passage of the Suez Canal. As we docked the ship was surrounded by small 'bumboats' trying to get us to part with our money for trinkets of very little value. The boatmen would throw a line upwards to the deck rail. Caught by a soldier the bargaining would begin along with a tug of war trying to relieve the boatman of his line and basket – to the accompaniment of various expletives both Egyptian and British. Before the gangway was in position the Ship's Provo Marshal issued his warning over the ship's Tannoy, 'Remember, men, it's backs to the wall today!' Port Said was not an attractive place and even then we were subject to a lot of abuse from local folk as we walked the streets. Having taken our pilot on board we set sail down the Canal. Passing sleek feluccas with their graceful single sails and occasional palm trees on the banks as El Kantara and Ismailia passed by, it was another special experience for me. Those names brought to life some of the World War I stories my father had told me when he was part of General Allenby's Palestine Campaign in 1916–18.

Next port of call was Aden, then a coaling station and a commercial centre. My cousin Joan's husband, Alan, was based there and came aboard and took me off for a quick look ashore. Colombo, Ceylon, was the next stop with a day's shore leave. Ashore and a trip to Mount Lavinia for the first decent swim since leaving the UK was marred by the unwanted attentions of young boys offering the services of their sisters.

So six weeks after leaving Liverpool, having travelled all the way at a speed of about 12 to 15 knots, we docked in Singapore. After disembarking with my steel trunk – mandatory for sea travel in those days – I arrived at Nee Soon Transit Camp. It was then commanded by Major Casey Petrie of the Gordons. A bluff, large and warm-hearted man, he gave me an equally warm welcome to the steamy heat of South-East Asia. We must have looked a very pallid bunch, well described by John Scurr in his book *Jungle Campaign, a memoir of National Service in Malaya 1949–51*, who had just arrived at Nee Soon en route from 'up-country' to board HMT *Empire Pride* for his return to the UK.

> From Singapore station we were transported to Nee Soon transit camp, a huge sprawling complex of buildings and tents. There were drafts of young lads there, newly arrived from Blighty, waiting to go up-country. I couldn't believe how white their skins were. They looked really sickly. 'Don't they look awful!' I said to Johnny Ainsworth. 'Surely we didn't use to look like that?'
> 'Oh yes we did!' Johnny assured me.

CHAPTER 4

Malaya

IN EARLY 1942 THE 2ND BATTALION, The Gordon Highlanders was part of the British forces defending the 'stronghold' of Singapore from attack by the Japanese forces coming south down the Malayan peninsula after their successful invasion in the north. The Gordons had retreated from original positions further north as the Japanese had fought their way towards Singapore Island. On 15 February Singapore surrendered to the victorious Japanese – one of the most devastating defeats suffered by the British Army during World War II.

That surrender led to the imprisonment of thousands of British service personnel, as well as civilians, in the most barbarous conditions endured by POWs in any theatre of war, conditions that were certainly considerably worse in terms of physical and mental torture and abuse than those suffered by my brother in his nearly two years incarceration as a German POW in the Germans' high security prison camp for Allied aircrew at Stalag Luft III in Sagan, Silesia.

Along with the remainder of the British forces in Singapore the 2nd Gordons became prisoners of the Japanese, imprisoned in the infamous Changi Jail. Many were forced to work on the Burma 'Railway'. These prisoners had to wait four long agonising years for liberation in 1946, until the dropping of atom bombs on Hiroshima and Nagasaki by the American Air Force brought a swift surrender by the Japanese.

Meanwhile across the Causeway in Malaya during these years of Japanese occupation Colonel F. Spencer Chapman DSO and his newly formed Force 132 were developing guerilla jungle warfare skills, training local Chinese, Malayan and Tamil left-wing guerillas and becoming a serious irritant to the occupying Japanese Army.

In his book *The Jungle is Neutral*, Chapman describes Force 132's campaign well. From his description one realises that, along with developing a local force of skilled jungle guerrilla fighters who successfully harassed the Japanese, we were also shipping in arms and other hardware to support them. So by the time the war ended in 1946, an effective network of predominantly Communist jungle fighters was in position with hidden arms dumps available to them. And they still nurtured designs to establish a Communist state in Malaya. A number of these 'freedom fighter heroes' even marched in the 1946 Victory Parades in Kuala Lumpur and London.

By 1948 Intelligence was indicating that this terrorist movement was likely to launch a concerted effort to achieve its goal of the overthrow of the Colonial Power and the local Malayan Administration. In June 1948 British Security Forces and the local police and Malayan Military mounted an operation to take all known terrorists into custody. But, too late, the hard core terrorists had already disappeared back into the jungle to 'resume operations', i.e. to launch their campaign of terror and extortion on the local population in the country's towns, villages, and outlying settlements (kampongs) – mostly populated by Malayan Chinese.

Thus the Malayan Emergency was proclaimed and an anti-terrorist campaign was launched to rid Malaya of the cancer of terrorism and allow an independent, democratic and multi-racial Malaya to emerge. Racial tensions had always been close to the surface. Immigrant Chinese were well established in the trade and commerce of the country; people of Tamil origin provided much of the labour that toiled on the rubber estates and in tin mines. The majority of the mining operations were foreign owned and located in the western half of the peninsula, where their telltale 'tailings' populated chunks of the skyline. The rubber estates, also with a high proportion of foreign ownership – much of it British – were scattered over the eastern side of the mountain range that ran down the backbone of the peninsula.

In the early years of the Emergency, the terrorists – or 'bandits' as they were now called – clearly had the upper hand despite the then best efforts of the authorities. On 6 October 1951 bandits had ambushed and killed Sir Henry Gurney, the British High Commissioner, near Kuala Lumpur.

Forty-eight hours after my arrival at Nee Soon Transit Camp I boarded a Chinese coastal freighter for the two-day sea trip up the east coast of Malaya to Kuantan in the state of Pahang, where I joined the 1st Battalion of the Gordon Highlanders. 1 Gordons was commanded by a 'wonderful wee man' – Lieutenant Colonel W.D.H. Duke MC. 'Dukie' had been among 2nd Battalion Gordons captured at the fall of Singapore in 1941. Taken prisoner by the

Japanese he had worked on the railway. A short and dapper man with clipped military moustache, he had a sharp eye for discipline and was very encouraging to new young subalterns like me. Also joining 1 Gordons was Ian Martineau, newly commissioned from RMA Sandhurst, who had travelled out with me on the *Empire Pride*.

We were both joined by newly arrived Jocks to undergo jungle training before posting to our companies. First night in the jungle was another memorable experience – akin to trying to get to sleep in a pitch-dark Piccadilly Circus. Noise from monkey calls, rattling cicadas and buzzing mosquitoes along with the momentary flashes of light from fireflies took some getting used to, quite aside from the possibility of a bandit lurking close by in the dense, smelly, damp undergrowth!

We always had a 'Crash Section' standing by in case of a sudden outbreak of bandit action near to camp. This section consisted of a GMC 15 cwt. truck and a Scout armoured car with a Bren gun mounted on the turret manned by a section of Jocks armed with rifles, Sten guns and a 2" mortar and grenades. During my first week at Kuantan the call came through about an incident several miles away. I was detailed to join the section. Riding in the GMC we had travelled some distance from camp when suddenly there was a double bump under both sets of wheels. We had obviously run over something in the pitch darkness.

We stopped and got out on to the road, unsure whether it was a booby trap of some kind. It was in fact the dead body of a Tamil rubber tapper who had been hacked to death with a tapper's knife – a vicious six to eight inch long knife with a sharp curled end used to cut a strip of bark on the latex-yielding panel in the trunk of a rubber tree. He had been taken out by bandits as a warning to other would-be informers. Needless to say not a pleasant sight but a sobering warning to me that we were up against a ruthless and cowardly enemy. There were no Marquess of Queensberry rules in this campaign.

Jungle training consisted of being taught and practising the technique of laying ambushes, patrolling and jungle craft – in other words how to live and operate in dense jungle (*ulu*) and savannah (*lallang*), building overnight shelters (*bashas*) from cut saplings tied with creepers and protected from rain by the poncho cape that each of us carried. Greater luxury could be achieved by the use of cut palm fronds as a kind of soft mattress. We were issued with a piece of face netting that could be soaked in the foul sickly smelling army issue mosquito repellent and then thrown over your face to keep the little buzzing buggers away from your flesh. We also each carried a toggle rope, which came in useful if you started to get into difficulties crossing swamps etc. as you could either be pulled to safety or another toggle added to give more rope – literally! Perhaps one of the most important pieces of advice given was never to look *at* the jungle undergrowth but always to look *through* it. Amazingly, this difference gave you a degree of extra vision and thus gave you a better chance of seeing lurking danger.

Among the other tricks learned was how to cope with all sizes of leech. Whenever you were near to or wading in water – swamps, streams, rivers – these bloodsuckers would find their way on to the most precious parts of your body as well as any exposed flesh, like arms, chest etc. Once arrived they would dig in and suck blood – a few drops in the case of small leeches or up to a cupful when a bull leech got to work. Typically all this was going on without the victim realising what was happening. Often the first indication of trouble

Somewhere in Pahang State, Malaya, 1 Gordons 1951. (L to r) John Biddlecombe, Jim Clarkson, David Ogilvie Stewart, RDF, David Saunders

was a sudden feeling of a trickle of blood where there shouldn't be, or catching sight of a bloated dark red body somewhere on your person. Despite crafty efforts to outwit the leech such as trouser tops carefully tucked into tightly tied canvas jungle boots, cigarette butts also stuffed into those tucks, they would still find a way in. The antidote was usually a touch from a lighted cigarette. The leech would fall off without leaving its jaw in you, thus avoiding possible infection and sores if you pulled them off, when their jaws would remain with you!

In the heat and humidity of the jungle dehydration was a real danger, which could lead to collapse as a result of excessive perspiration. The antidote was two or three salt tablets and a gulp of water from your water bottle. Shortly thereafter you would be back on your feet. So we carried salt tablets and also Paludrine tablets as protection against malaria. When out on patrol I used to hold a Paludrine parade at sunrise to ensure that every one of us swallowed the daily pill. I required movement of the Adam's apple as evidence of pill taken!

Moving around in dense jungle was akin to navigation at sea. Most of the time you could not see more than a few yards around you. So understanding of and expert use of a compass was essential on operations to find your way both to particular objectives and to geographic features. It was also vital if on a joint patrol with other units to avoid inadvertently making contact with the other unit and opening fire with potentially disastrous results. Some other units' map reading and patrol discipline was worse than others. Consequently, when I led my platoon out on patrol I would always check beforehand that no other units were operating in the same area. Then, if you did have a contact, you could assume that it was unfriendly and react accordingly. It was not unusual, occasionally, to be unsure of where you were; you would never admit to being lost! On such occasions you looked for help to your Ibans. Ibans were headhunters from Borneo enlisted by the army as expert jungle trackers. Their main task was to look out for signs of bandit movement, tracks etc., and so help a patrol to make contact with and ideally kill bandits. Dark-skinned tough little men with pierced dangling ear lobes, tattoos and long black hair, they usually carried a *panga* (long knife) and often a blowpipe used to kill small animals to cook. Four Ibans were attached to my platoon, Ajah Anak Nyangai, Embuas Anak Apol, Ayom Anak Ungang and Bada Anak Usa.

Usually I took two of them out with me on patrol. So when I was unsure as to where I was – usually when we were trying to find an RV with transport to return to Sungkai – I would tell them to lead us home. They had an uncanny ability which most times worked well. However, after several months of patrolling, my Jocks and I had also picked up basic skills of identifying signs of movement and the direction of travel they indicated – a boot print, a broken twig still damp with sap, a torn hanging creeper. On occasion they could tell you to go in the opposite direction to that indicated by the signs, I suppose either to avoid trouble or to get to camp quicker. I would then 'correct' them. They were very particular about personal hygiene and each evening when we had set up camp they would go off to the nearby watering point for their ablutions. One evening with the light fading suddenly all hell let loose with rapid fire from the Bren gunner on sentry duty and everyone hitting the deck either half dressed or searching for their weapon.

Then back into camp came our two very frightened Ibans. Our sentry had heard movement outside the perimeter and assuming it was bandits had fired off nearly a whole magazine in his anxiety. From that moment on I issued orders that no-one was to ever move anywhere in camp without his weapon at his side, as part of the panic had been caused by men wandering and chatting without their weapon with them. Such is the way that lessons are learned.

All insects in Malaya seemed to be three to four times larger than their British equivalents. Soldier ants, preying mantises, and large red ants – oh how they could bite! – along with gorgeously coloured moths and butterflies and sticky viscous spiders' webs that gave you quite a surprise if you inadvertently walked into one – all were a botanist's delight, but all of them unwanted accompaniments to patrols and ambushes.

Finally in August, I joined A Company commanded by Major George Elsmie, a Burma Railway veteran, and took command of Number 1 Platoon. Our Headquarters was a vacated planter's bungalow close to the main road near Sungkai in the state of Perak. I and the three other company officers lived in the bungalow, with the Company Office next door and NCOs and Jocks housed in tents some distance away.

Late one evening, some days after my arrival, the compound suddenly came under automatic fire. Taking cover behind the

Dinner is served! On patrol near Sungkai, Perak State, Malaya 1952

bungalow's balcony I found myself lying beside our Company
Sergeant Major, CSM 'Snowy' Strachan. In broad Doric he muttered
to me: 'It's me thirty ninth f——g birthday today and it's nae goin'
tae be me last!' We survived and the sudden firing ceased as suddenly
as it had begun – source still unknown. Our sole entertainment at
Sungkai was an old wind-up His Master's Voice gramophone kindly
donated to us by the Aberdeen WVS. With the gramophone they had
sent old 78 records of well-known operatic pieces etc. – just the thing
for homesick Jocks and the rest of us! On a Friday evening – pay day
– I was doing Orderly Officer duty and time had come to close down
the tented bar. Having done so I became aware of the sound of
'Manina Frigida' from *La Bohème* being sung by Benjamino Gigli
wafting across the moonlit jungle air. It was coming from across the
compound at one end of the balcony of the bungalow. I came round
the corner of the balcony to see two members of my platoon, both
draped over the lid of the gramophone and with tears flowing
unashamedly down their cheeks and obviously foo. I asked the
inevitable question: 'What's the matter with you two?' Their
unforgettable reply came back: 'We dinna ken the tune, Sirr, but it's
making us f——g miserable!'

Regular patrols were the order of the day along with laying night and first light ambushes. Patrols lasted from two days to over two weeks if deep penetration into the jungle was required. Most operations were based on information from the local Malay police or local informers on bandit movements – much of it unreliable but usually followed up on the off-chance of a contact. On one occasion, acting on information that a particular track was to be used by several bandits on the move, I took one section of six men (my platoon Corporal Coates and five Jocks). We were dropped off from our three-ton wagon near the area the day before the promised day. We moved a good way in on the edge of the rubber estate where it met thick jungle undergrowth. I laid out our ambush with the Bren gun at one end covering the length of the ambush alley and the remainder of us spread out in positions over about 50 yards. By first light nothing had been seen; then suddenly the Bren opened up – several short bursts – and then silence. After a short wait to see if there were any further developments, quietly and on our agreed signal, I raised the ambush and crept up to the Bren gun position. Private Dickson, the Bren gunner, said, 'I couldn't make it out. Suddenly I saw one bandit coming straight toward me. I held my fire until he was almost upon me and then let him have it!' Unknowingly, Dickson had been sitting virtually on top of a load of hidden rice waiting to be picked up by the dead bandit! He was also carrying a roll of canvas presumably to be used for making their uniforms. Later I took it to the Regimental tailor who made up a pair of excellent highland gaiters for me that I later used on full dress occasions.

This contact was typical of the war in Malaya – short sharp contacts, a brief firefight, sometimes with a result and sometimes not as one's adversaries often just melted back into impenetrable jungle even when apparently the recipients of many rounds of ammunition. So there was a lot of time patrolling with little or no action. Keeping one's Jocks alert and at the ready as well as oneself was therefore a real challenge. The price of lack of vigilance was high. In February 1952 a British Board of Directors visiting one of their rubber plantations on Narborough Estate near Sungkai was attacked by bandits and suffered severe casualties including several deaths. 1 Platoon and 2 Platoon under command of my chum Ken Rose were sent out to track down and kill the killers. I was patrolling on one side of the main road and Ken had taken the other side. We each set up our platoon camps. On the third day of searching the area Ken and his section were returning to their base using the same track they had used on the previous two days.

Bandits must have watched them. They were ambushed and all seven of them were killed on 17 February 1952. This was an absolute tragedy and the loss of a good friend and six irreplaceable Jocks, a mix of National Servicemen and Regulars – Second Lieutenant Ken Rose, L/Cpl Learmouth and Ptes Fairgrieve, Mackenzie, Nutt, K. Wright and P. Wright. It was a chilling reminder of the axiom about patrolling: 'Never use the same route twice.' As headline news in the UK it brought General Gerald Templer, by then Supreme Commander in Malaya after Gurney's assassination, to the scene. I was greatly impressed by his attitude and concern for detail as Captain Jim Robertson and I showed him the carefully prepared and well-concealed ambush positions used by the bandits.

Also in February 1952, King George VI died. We were instructed to stop for two minutes' silence – wherever you were on patrol in ambush or off duty – and wear black armbands.

2nd Lieutenant Ken Rose at A Company HQ, 1 Gordons, Sungkai.
Killed in action 17 February 1952

All that did we do.

Shortly afterwards, I went down to Singapore for four days' leave with John Comyn, another National Service Officer. We stayed at the Adelphi Hotel and were able to enjoy the blissful coolness of the Grill Room at the Raffles Hotel, then the only air conditioned spot on the island other than the Hong Kong & Shanghai Bank Branch on Colliers Quay!

Before I left the UK my Uncle Nicol, an Aberdonian who had spent most of his life in the Far East with my Aunt Edith, my mother's eldest sister − the opera singer − as a Director of a cold storage business, gave me a 'letter of introduction' to some old friends in Singapore. I contacted them and was asked to join them at their club for cocktails. I arrived and was handed a stenghah (gin and tonic). I realised very quickly that as a mere young army officer who was risking his neck in a war to prevent terrorists up-country actually disturbing their well ordered way of life, I was not quite but nearly some lower form of life in which they showed very little interest! It was not what I had expected. Perhaps it was too swift a contrast for me after the sweat and filth of jungle living. I found it hard to understand at the time and as I look back on the incident now it represents to me the outdated and snobbish face of old British colonialism − hopefully long since gone.

By the time of the new Queen's Birthday, 1 Gordons had moved to Selarang Barracks in Singapore for retraining and ceremonial duties. I was put in command of a detachment of 1 Gordons sent up to Kuala Lumpur to take part in the Queen's Birthday Parade on the Padang in front of the Club and Post Office. Highland Regiments normally march at 110 paces per minute. Unfortunately our detachment was placed behind the Gurkhas who, as light infantry, march at 140 paces per minute. It really did not work out too well for either the Gordons or the Gurkhas!

Life in Selarang Barracks was very different to hacking through dense jungle day after day up-country in Malaya. Along with the other subalterns I was on parade at 0600 hrs to have my Highland dancing steps brought up to standard under the eagle eye of Pipe Major Anderson. Pipie Anderson had piped the 51st Highland Division into battle at El Alamein. To him I owe any skill I retain in the Highland Fling, Gillie Cullum (Solo Sword Dance) and the Foursome Reel. We were passed out as fit to dance on Regimental

'A Gay Gordon'; ready for a Regimental Guest Night, Officers' Mess, 1 Gordons, Selarang Barracks, Singapore 1952

Guest Nights, which actually were great fun and imbued one with a further sense of pride in being a Gordon.

On 6 July 1952 I went to Singapore Station to say goodbye to 1 Gordons as the Battalion departed back up-country to Tampin to resume anti-terrorist operations. Any sadness was more than offset the following day when I boarded the ill-fated HMT *Windrush* to sail home and be demobilised and return to civvy street. Even then this 15,000-ton troopship was experiencing engine failures. We lost engine power for about two days in the Sumatra Straits but survived a massive storm as we crossed the Indian Ocean. It was a more leisurely trip back to the UK than the journey out, possibly because most of the passengers were, like me, at the end of regular service. On the last night on board before docking at Southampton a fancy dress party was held. I have long since forgotten what I went as but I well remember one bright spark who wore his jungle greens with a large red circular patch on his backside. He had gone as a stuffed olive – no doubt such imagination has rewarded him well in the intervening years! HMT *Windrush* went on fire and sank off the island of Panteleria in the Mediterranean on its next round trip.

After disembarkation I travelled by train up to Aberdeen and reported to Regimental Headquarters at Bridge of Don Barracks to await demobilisation. In a couple of days all was done and I was asked to accompany a newly commissioned National Service Second Lieutenant on his way to London and onwards to join 1 Gordons at Tampin, Malaya. His name was David Macmillan who was to become one of my greatest friends over a lifetime of fun and hilarious occasions. It started as it was to continue. We boarded the overnight sleeper in Aberdeen and took our place in one of the old four-berth carriages with the upper berth slung by chains from the roof. We were joined by one other man in the compartment. We prepared for bed, David kindly letting me borrow his kilt to add to my own as a blanket – I was still feeling the cold after such warm climes. Then to our surprise, our travelling companion undressed and unstrapped and hung up what turned out to be his wooden leg! On arrival in London the next morning the contraption was donned again and off he went. An unforgettable way to start a lifelong friendship that sadly ended with his sudden death on a business trip in Lithuania on the day of the official opening of the Gordon Highlanders Museum by HRH Prince Charles in Aberdeen some 43 years later.

Everyone's National Service commitment included a further 3½ years of service in the Territorial Army. So I was posted to 4/7th Gordons, then based at Woolmanhill in Aberdeen, for occasional drills and annual two-week camps, of which more later. Back home I readied myself to go up to Emmanuel College in early October to re-start my academic life, and enjoy a happy reunion with Una and my father.

National Service gave me an unforgettable two years' experience in a number of ways. It provided the opportunity to experience active service in a crack Highland Regiment. It also allowed me to participate, as one of the many service personnel together with the Gurkhas and Malaya Police, in beating one of the most lethal terrorist organisations of its time. At the close of this campaign in 1962, Malaya moved on to become a stable country which, after a short-lived liaison with the City State of Singapore, became an important part of what is now known as Malaysia. I know it sounds hackneyed to describe it this way, but it did make men out of boys and was a real force for greater social cohesion in later years based on the experience gained in very unusual circumstances. As a National Service Lieutenant, I owed a great deal to my NCOs, particularly Sergeant Joe Stacey. Originally a Black Watch soldier, he had been posted to the Gordons and was a great backstop for me from time to time, ensuring that, when appropriate, more seasoned and better judgement prevailed! I also made lifelong friends of many of my fellow officers along with an equally enduring association with the Gordon Highlanders. I suppose in the modern jargon it provided a most unusual pair of 'gap years'!

My TA service was also memorable, although in a rather different way because I was not resident in the regimental area as I was by then up at Emmanuel College commencing my studies. David Macmillan, also at Cambridge, and I were therefore transferred to the London Scottish for our attendance at mandatory drill nights and weekends. Despite my obvious affiliations with that TA regiment, for reasons that I cannot explain, neither David nor I felt comfortable in their Mess – perhaps it was their attitude towards us as away from home Gordons. We shall never know. After some six months or so, with the help of chums in the 4/7th we managed to be transferred back to the 4/7 Gordons for Annual Camp attendance.

My then employer allowed one to take two weeks' extra leave to attend camp in addition to normal holiday leave without any reduction in salary. So, provided that after payment of my Mess bill I could take a balance home to add to the housekeeping, Una acquiesced. In 1956 the Duke of Gloucester, the late King's brother, was our Colonel-in-Chief and was to present new colours to the battalion on Harlaw Field in Aberdeen. Needless to say, two weeks' camp allowed adequate practice for the Colours Parade – virtually the equivalent to the Trooping of the Colour Parade that takes place each summer in London to mark the monarch's official birthday. Jack Harper, then in charge of Scottish Television, was our commanding officer and also parade commander. It required him to call out over sixty drill orders – needless to say all of us behind him were hoping that he would shout his orders in the correct sequence. To get it wrong would have caused chaos.

In preparation for the day, a new loo had been installed in the Mess for royal use and all officers had been instructed to acquire a pair of decent looking brown leather gloves to wear on parade. Come the day, we are formed up ready to march on to Harlaw Field. Suddenly another officer appears, probably the good Duke's equerry, and has a quick conversation with Jack Harper. Then comes the order: 'Remove gloves and pass them down the line – the Duke has forgotten his'; and he did not use the loo either! The parade was a great success culminating with the battalion marching down Union Street with fixed bayonets, new colours flying and pipes and drums doing us proud – a memorable moment.

Usually during each camp an exercise would be mounted to test our military skills and tactical awareness. One year our task was to land on the Isle of Arran and fight through the island to remove alien forces that had taken over the island. We boarded landing craft on the mainland and disembarked at Brodick on Arran. So far so good, but as we started on our three-day exercise our fortunes changed. First it was the weather which turned from clouds to torrential horizontal driving rain. Next it soon became obvious that our exercise referee, a Major Duffin of the Scots Guards and a Regular army officer, was going to make sure we came under serious attack.

I was then battalion machine gun officer in which role I had to stay close to my CO, Jack Harper. As Major Duffin announced that we were under attack from a flank, Jack would call up a rifle company to deal with the opposition. All the time the rain was soaking everyone. Once again Major Duffin reported we were now under artillery barrage from a point to our east. Again, Jack ordered a rifle company to deal with the situation. And so it went on. Finally Major Duffin, clearly exasperated that we were either not taking the exercise seriously enough or not showing acceptable tactical discipline, could contain himself no longer. Within earshot of me he asked Jack Harper: 'Excuse me, sir, but where are you getting all these rifle companies from?' Jack's reply was typical of the man and why we all had such great affection and respect for him. 'The same place as you are getting these ruddy attacks that are stopping us from getting home and in the dry. Away with you and let's get home and dry!'

Poor Duffin's frustrations did not end there. The following day, after a night drying out in nearby farm buildings, the battalion departed by vehicle for Lamlash where a landing craft was due to take us off to return to the mainland. There had been no let-up in the weather and the rain continued to pelt down. We arrived at Lamlash hard to await the landing craft. It appeared and was obviously finding difficulty in docking, despite Duffin's frantic signs to the captain of the landing craft. So finally, in desperation, Major Duffin waded into the water to help guide the craft in. Finally all was well, we embarked, and a memorable but not untypical TA exercise was over.

It was our custom in the 4/7th Gordons to dine out officers who were either retiring or leaving the battalion onwards to another posting. We were dining out Major Ralph Nickson, a regular officer with whom many of us had served. After dinner a loving cup concoction was prepared and passed around all present. It was so positioned that Ralph would be the last to imbibe and by custom drain the cup. Major Duffin was with us. When the cup was passed to him he commented, 'We only drink champagne in the Guards.' The 51st Highland Division has always reckoned that it had no equal in the British Army, including the Brigade of Guards. Thus it was not surprising that his comment should not pass without response. Two junior officers quietly left the room, to appear a few moments later bearing a silver salver on which was placed a bottle of champagne. They went up to Major Duffin and in the best military style said, 'Now drink that you . . .!'

CHAPTER 5

'Salad Days' at Emmanuel College – Cambridge

IN 1952 JULIAN SLADE AND Dorothy Reynolds were enjoying well-earned West End success with their musical entertainment *Salad Days*, a nice light-hearted musical typical of the pleasant, well-ordered lifestyle of that era, before the 60s arrived to shatter so much of what had been a good mixture of common sense, sensibility, and the nurturing of tradition and strong family values.

At Cambridge University in October 1952 the majority of the undergraduate body had completed National Service except for those in specialist disciplines such as medicine and dentistry who would do their National Service after completion of their studies. Thus I suppose they were able to provide qualified personnel for service duties in those disciplines.

I think that by today's standards as I observe them we were a fairly sober, straight-laced and disciplined bunch. Tweed sports jackets, corduroy trousers, flat cap and clean shoes along with shirt and tie were the norm. And, of course, then it was largely a male only institution, except for Girton and Newnham Colleges. College gates closed at 10 p.m. Ladies and girlfriends were allowed to be in College rooms up to 11 p.m. only. So any 'after-hours' arrivals or departures had to be made over the College wall. This was a highly dangerous exercise at Emmanuel, as it required safe passage along the top of a narrow wall beside a glass-roofed bath house. Any slippage as a result of drink or a misplaced foot would land one straight through glass into a very large bath. Such was the environment that I entered when I went up to Emmanuel College in October 1952 to read Economics.

The discipline of learning at Cambridge was, and I presume still is, subtle. There was no requirement to attend lectures but it was wise and helpful to do so. About every ten days or so supervision sessions with one's Director of Studies who might possibly also be one's Tutor helped sort out the general course of your studies and where you would go for additional supervision with Tutors and Fellows, some of whom would be in Colleges other than your own. Teaching was by way of lectures, background reading followed by a presentation, and group discussion of essays prepared in advance of tutorial sessions on facets of one's subject. The daunting part of these sessions was that they were also attended by three or four of one's fellow undergraduates, thus to appear totally unprepared really was not good strategy.

All of this was set against the temptations of the array of interests waiting to be exploited, at both College and University level – music, the arts, sport, politics et al.

The subtlety of all this was that the onus lay on the individual student to sort out his (or her) priorities and to manage his time accordingly so that at the end of the academic year he could deliver an exam result that was good enough to enable him to qualify for the first part of the Tripos and thus qualify to move onto the second and final part one or two years later to complete the final part of the Tripos and secure his Degree: all in all a great training for later life in the organisation of work and pleasure and the competing interests they represent for most of us.

So, in addition to my study of Economics, I pitched in to several other activities. Based on my KGS First Eleven hockey background I was occasionally invited to play for the College Eleven. I tried out with the College Boat Club and secured a place in the first eight in the Fairburn, Lent and May races – a place I occupied until in 1954/5 I felt I had to devote more time to my studies. In 1952/3 Tony Leadley was Captain of the Emmanuel Boat Club and along with Louis McCagg, Emmanuel's 1952 Harvard scholar, raced in that year's Blue Boat under the presidency of Geoffrey Crowden of Pembroke College. Leadley re-took his seat at 6 in the 1953 1st May Boat. I rowed at bow in that boat. We bumped Clare 1st Boat on day one. We came very close to bumping Jesus College on Grassy Corner on the third night.

Bumping racing is an exhausting discipline. You have two or three opportunities owing to the bends in the River Cam at which time you make your bid to bump. Peter Tetley, our cox, was totally overcome when, having ordered us to put in the necessary spurt to catch Jesus as they inevitably slowed their speed to go round the bend, our bow just missed the Jesus's rudder. The consequence was to place us at a severe disadvantage, as we would therefore have to

Emmanuel College First May Boat closing in on Clare College First May Boat at Grassy Corner before making a bump in the Plough Reach, May Bumping Races on the River Cam, 1953. RDF at Bow

take the bend wide, providing a greater advantage to the crew coming at us from behind.

My other great pleasure was participating in the Emmanuel Singers. Run by the College Dean, Hugh Burnaby, a small number of Gilbert and Sullivan enthusiasts gathered in the Dean's rooms on Monday evenings after dinner in Hall. Once there we were served port and sang various excerpts from Gilbert and Sullivan operas. Dean Burnaby fashioned these into what he called 'exkerps'. These exkerps were then presented at the annual Emmanuel College concert to 'rave reviews'. John Britten, the nephew of Benjamin the well-known composer, Nigel Ward and I rendered a very memorable 'Three Little Maids' from *The Mikado*.

I found economics a strange discipline. To my mind much of what I was being taught and was learning seemed to me to be a rather complex mathematical presentation of the blindingly obvious. For example 'the law of diminishing returns': in lay terms, 'when it gets to the point where the extra ounce of effort delivers less than an extra ounce of benefit, the law has been well illustrated.' The more exact scientific definition goes along the lines of, 'when the cost of the incremental unit of output is equal to or greater than the unit revenue from that incremental unit of output, the point of diminishing return has been reached'!

Nevertheless there were memorable highlights during my first year's study; one of them was to attend the Marshall Lecture. In 1953 it was delivered by the then 90-year-old Professor Pigou whose book *The Economics of Welfare* was, and may still be as far as I know, the standard work on the subject. A tall, gaunt figure in black gown, it was an occasion to be remembered. Maurice Dobb, another eminent academic, lectured us on wages and social economics. An ardent left-winger, he was not amused when, after Stalin's death, we all attended his lecture at the Mill Road Lecture Rooms wearing bright red ties!

Readers will therefore understand why I changed over to read law at the end of my first year at Emmanuel. That change required me to come up to College for a 'long vacation term' in the summer of 1953. Its purpose was to enable me to catch up on parts of the syllabus taken by the first year law students. Fortunately it did not require me to include Roman Law or Jurisprudence.

1953 was the Festival of Britain Year and a Regatta was organised on the Serpentine in London. I had been elected Captain of the Emmanuel Boat Club and, along with John Bunn, who had come up to Emmanuel from Latymer Upper School at the same time as I, we decided to enter the double sculls event at that Regatta. To allow us to get our 30-foot long racing shell and two pairs of sculls there, we enlisted the help of a fellow Emmanuel undergraduate, Peter McAlister. Peter owned a venerable old Rover saloon car. So with a frame fixed up over the bonnet with the help of the College carpenter, the shell and sculls were loaded onto the roof and we set off for London. All went well until we reached the Old Kent Road in rush hour early in the morning. In slow moving traffic the Rover finally sputtered and stopped and would not re-start, despite frantic efforts. I was in the passenger seat and Peter looked across and said, 'You will have to get out and check the battery.' The battery happened to be under my seat so I got out, put my seat on the pavement, removed the floorboard and there was the battery with one lead misplaced. Traffic by now had become impatient, horns were blasting. All was replaced and we got on our way and parked the car plus boat beside the Serpentine. As we were not due to race until late afternoon the three of us went off to see something of the town. We returned just after lunch to be met by the wrath of the Regatta Stewards who had been trying to get the car moved since shortly after our arrival. Little did they know that with one or two rockings from side to side the windows would have collapsed and they could then have manoeuvred the car out of the way! John and I lost our heat but it had been an unforgettable day, remembered only recently when Una, my wife, and I attended Peter's seventieth birthday celebration.

I enjoyed the law. My knowledge of Latin helped me unravel some of the more archaic dicta and I came to appreciate the way in which English Common Law had grown out of Case Law, along with the concept of equity – so absent in other legal systems where statute law rules supreme. By now I had changed Tutors and Fred Odgers was to look after me for the rest of my time at Emmanuel. A practising lawyer himself, I felt more at home under his tutelage and found his advice and judgement always helpful and realistic. Rowing was now occupying a large part of my non-academic time – up to 25–30 hours per week either on the water or coaching crews.

Trial by Jury exkerp was in preparation and I had joined the XII Club where I shared Membership with Tom King who had come up to Emmanuel in 1953 later to become an MP and a member of Margaret Thatcher's Government and now Lord King.

As Captain of Boats I was also a Member of the Emmanuel Lions Club – the gathering of College sports captains and College blues. My story from that involvement has already been told by Cecil Parkinson in his biography *Right at the Centre*. Cec was a Lions Club member by virtue of his Captaincy of the College Athletics Club. Vincent Lumsden, a cricket blue from Jamaica, was also a member of our Lions Club. At a particular meeting we were reviewing possible new members. Someone raised a question about the prevailing rules about 'blackballing'. 'Was it one or two?' Two black balls was the decision. At that moment Vin got up and with a very sombre, almost hurt expression on his black face left the room. Then the implication of our decision dawned on us and an embarrassed silence descended on everyone. To be broken a moment later when Vin re-entered the room with a very broad smile on his face – having thoroughly enjoyed our discomfiture.

The XII Club, Emmanuel College, Cambridge, 1954. (Back row) Tim Taylor, John Buckley, John Twallin, Nick Raffle, Nigel Ward. (Front row) John Griffiths, Enoch Hunt, RDF, Tom King, John Britten

When Douglas went up to Emmanuel in 1941 Edward Welbourne was Senior Tutor and Dean Burnaby was President of the Boat Club. When I went to Cambridge in November 1949 to sit my Previous Examination, Ted Welbourne had become Master and Peter Hunter Blair was Senior Tutor and had taken over from Burnaby as EBC President.

I sat History, English and Latin in the exam. Then came the interview with several Fellows which I remember I found quite daunting. Hunter Blair and the Master were placed opposite me when I entered the room. I cannot recall the details of that interview but I must have conducted myself reasonably well along with average but not outstanding exam results because shortly afterwards I received the good news that I had been awarded a place for entry in October 1952 after the completion of my National Service. Perhaps the spirit of my brother was watching over me.

Welbourne was a great and wise character to all of us. Wounded in the First World War and awarded the MC, he had a slight stoop and often an undergraduate would bump into him as he strolled in the college gardens dressed often in an old cardigan and battered hat and find himself engaged in discussion of a totally abstruse subject. It was not unknown for aspiring students to find themselves surprised at being interviewed by the person they had assumed to be one of the college gardeners. Endless stories have been told about him, some apocryphal and some true.

In 1954 the College Rugby Club had reached the Final of Cuppers (the Inter collegiate rugby competition). As Captain of Boats along with other sports captains and the Master and several Fellows, I was among the guests at the Club's annual dinner in the Old Library. It was a special year. The Fifteen was captained by Tommy McClung, a University Blue, to become an International and Captain of Scotland. Other team members included three other Blues; Nick Raffles, Alan Barter and Bill Downey. The atmosphere was suitably boisterous. By the time we took our seats most movable items such as bread rolls and condiments had found themselves used as missiles. The time came for speeches. When all seemed done suddenly a call went up for the Master to speak. Reluctantly he rose to his feet and started to speak. 'There are enough engineers present to know that well-oiled machinery runs quietly!' and sat down. It took a moment to realise that we would get no more words from Ted Welbourne that evening. It is a phrase that has helped me out on several occasions since!

May Balls were a very enjoyable part of the social scene at Cambridge and during my second year I became a member of the Emmanuel May Ball Committee. Aside from being involved in the planning and preparation for the College Ball, membership also entitled one to enjoy free tickets to several other College Balls. Each year Una would come up to Cambridge and I would arrange overnight lodgings for her over the Ball period. For the 1954 May Ball I had fixed lodgings in New Road for Una. I had carefully arranged with the landlady that the front door would not be locked so that when we returned early in the morning after festivities had ended and we'd completed the punt trip from Grantchester back to Cambridge Una could get in without difficulty. All went well until at about 4 a.m. Una in ballgown and I in black tie arrived at the front door to find it locked and bolted. Any amount of knocking and ringing of an exhausted wind-up bell had no effect. Nonplussed for a moment, I suddenly remembered that two other good girlfriends who had also been at the Ball had a flat in Lansfield Road. After throwing stones up at their second floor window they realised our problem and Una was safely ensconced for the rest of the night. I made my way back to Emmanuel over the normal route at that time of day – over the wall by the bath house, which I described earlier. The next challenge was to get Una's day clothes from her lodgings. To my relief when I turned up at about 8.30 a.m. to collect her clothes the landlady had to unlock the front door and realised the dilemma we had had to face!

From time to time Una would come up to Cambridge for a weekend visit. She would travel back to London on the 6 p.m. train from Cambridge station to Liverpool Street, better known as the 'Popsy Express'. So on the platform would assemble a number of undergraduates saying farewell to their girlfriends. However, attention to one's girlfriend tended to waver when Jonathan Miller was on the platform saying goodbye to his particular girlfriend. Usually decked out in shirt, jeans and sandals – pretty far out in those days – he had developed a technique of breathing on the train's window and writing sweet nothings in reverse to his lady within. This performance could at times be much more captivating than a farewell kiss to one's own girlfriend!

In 1954 Edward Oakden, another Emmanuel Boat Club Member, and I decided to try our hand at pair oar racing. We settled down well together and decided to enter the University Magdalene Pairs competition in the Easter Term. This was a timed race over the bumps course and required skill in steering the racing shell. This was done by means of two leather thongs each attached to the rudder. Each thong was also attached to one foot in the stretcher. This foot pivoted at the heel. So by moving the foot from one side to the other the rower could steer the shell. Over the three days of the competition Edward and I were surprised at our success. By relying on a strong spurt in both the Gut and the Plough Reach on the Cam course we managed to beat comfortably three other pairs comprised of Cambridge Blues. On the final evening going down to the start our rudder thong snapped. As 'steers' this was a particularly serious crisis for me. Our worthy boatman, George Hones, who always accompanied us on the bank, came to the rescue with a length of old telephone cord. Unfortunately it had no flexibility and was almost impossible to move in either direction by one's foot. As a result our hopes of winning the final were dashed. However, so emboldened we decided to enter for the Goblets at Henley in the summer.

Anyone familiar with the world of rowing will remember that 1954 was memorable as the year in which 'the Russians arrived'. In their blue trunks and red singlets with CCCP emblazoned upon them, they were impressive specimens. They were suspicious of their lodgings provided, so moved. They were suspicious of the length of the course, so they measured it to check. And it soon became obvious that they were a very different kind of opposition. For example in practice sessions in our eight, the Russian sculler *Tukalov* could easily stay with us. The Russian crews had entered virtually all the senior events at Henley so come the day Edward and I lined up at the start of our heat against two Oxford Blues – Messrs Clack and Christie. We did not have a good race and were beaten easily. However up against the Russian pair Buldakov and Ivanov in the final, Clack and Christie found themselves trailing by yards. As it was in the Goblets final so it was in the Grand Challenge Cup, the Visitors and the Diamond Sculls. All were won by a Russian crew who seemed to be not the slightest fatigued by their exertions. Their success had a very salutary effect on notions of training etc. amongst the British rowing fraternity, akin, in its way, to the effect that Russian Sputnik success had on energising US efforts in the space race. It contributed to a complete overhaul of and re-think in training methods for all Clubs, lessons that have been learned with great success over the years since then; perhaps epitomised by Sir Steven Redgrave's light fours crew record-breaking success in winning Olympic Gold in the 2000 Olympics at Sydney.

One of the great learning experiences and disciplines of life at Cambridge was the ultimate realisation that the securing of a degree overrode the enjoyment of all the other pastimes and pleasures available to you. So, having spent up to 30 hours a week either coaching crews or rowing myself, I decided in October 1954 that I had to concentrate on my studies. I withdrew from serious involvement in rowing for that year, except for a wonderful row in the Thames Head of the River Race in spring 1955. We started in 121st position and finished 19th.

During the long summer vacation in 1954 I decided to find temporary work to provide a little more pocket money to add to the

My last race for Emmanuel Boat Club, April 1955; passing under Hammersmith Bridge, Thames Head of the River Race

thirty shillings per week that I was living on. I was taken on by the LCC Parks Department as a gardener at £7.0s.0d. per week. Here I learned the art of mowing bowling greens and other skills. On arrival at the depot at 7.30 a.m. my gang was then delivered to the day's work location. Breakfast break at 8.30 and then back to work. It was here that I first experienced working to rule. On occasion it would rain. Our foreman, Bert, would call us in to shelter under a nearby tree. Bert would not allow work to resume until he had applied his rain test. He would place a cigarette paper in the palm of his hand, walk out from under the tree and, with palm outstretched slowly count up to five. Work would not resume until there was not a single drop of rain on the paper by the count of five.

I was fully aware that a first class degree was definitely beyond my likely attainment but I was determined to do my best. As the date of

Finals neared I decided to analyse the previous ten years' Part II Law Tripos Examination Papers to decide on a likely mix of subjects that I should concentrate on. This effort paid dividends, with one exception. The Law Faculty decided to change its focus in the Criminal Law Paper. In company with a number of my fellow undergraduates — and supported by Freddie Odgers our tutor — we believed it pulled us all down a class in the final result. Nevertheless come Degree day I found myself in the Procession at the Senate House where I was led by the hand to receive my Degree on bended knee from the Vice-Chancellor of the University.

During the last half of my final year, as with others, I had concentrated, with help from the University Appointments Board, on trying to find suitable employment for when I came down in summer 1955. I had no serious intention of taking my Law studies further either to practise as a solicitor or to seek to be called to the Bar.

Graduation Day. I receive my BA Degree at the Senate House, Cambridge,
25 June 1955

I firmly believed that I would find a career in business, although at that point I wasn't really sure what the word meant. So interviews were arranged for me with a number of major companies including Unilever, Socony Vacuum (now Mobil Oil) – and the Metal Box Company. The last was memorable as both Cecil Parkinson and I were due to go forward for interview with that company at the same time. Unfortunately, on the day before our interviews, I went down with flu and had to cancel my appointment. Cecil Parkinson went forward to that interview and secured the job. I have often pondered subsequently where our different careers might have ended up had the chances been reversed!

I was finally offered a position as a management trainee with Socony Vacuum at a salary of £450 per annum and started work in their Head Offices in Tothill Street in London in September 1955. So started a 43-year career in business, which was to take me around the world and into positions of major responsibility in two world class institutions – McKinsey & Company and the H. J. Heinz Company.

CHAPTER 6

The Business World Beckons

MY ONLY EXPOSURE TO BUSINESS BEFORE September 1955 had
been occasional visits to my father's factory where he directed
a workforce that produced telecommunications equipment such as
telephones, telephone exchanges, and after the War consumer items
such as vacuum cleaners, irons and the like. I well remember his
frustration and anger at having to deal with strikes among some
sections of his workforce during the War.

On arrival at the Socony Vacuum offices in Tothill Street, I met
three gentlemen who were to be my colleagues for the next two years
as fellow management trainees: Malcolm Burr whom I was to meet
again when I was leading a McKinsey study at Internal Distillers and
Vintners in the 1970s, Larry Rogers and Richard Stopford. Interestingly, within six to ten years of our joining we had all departed to
build our careers elsewhere. Nevertheless I believe we all benefited
from spending nearly two years working in all functions of that oil
company. Four weeks at the new Coryton Refinery in the Thames
Estuary tutored us in the process of converting crude oil into various
elements of petroleum products from jet fuel to bitumen. A stint at
the Barrel Cleaning Department in Wandsworth was an experience
akin to Army basic training followed by several weeks work in the
Birkenhead Oil Blending & Greasemaking Plant. This was particularly interesting as it was a time when experimentation was under
way to replace the conventional time honoured traditions of testing
grease mixes manually to establish correct consistency etc. with
computer operation, to the great consternation of the then Quality
Control personnel.

After Birkenhead it was across to Sunderland and four weeks at a
distribution terminal. Here we experienced the world of the tanker
driver and the back-up distribution system needed to provide service
to customers ranging from industrial companies through commercial,
industrial customers to retail gas stations. This was followed by four
weeks at the Retail Training School outside Birmingham where I
received my first tip from a motorist who seemed to be well satisfied

with the four point service that I gave him in the days before self-service overtook the forecourt.

Una and I had decided to get engaged in 1955 and held our engagement party in Chapman's Garden at Emmanuel. One of my goals in starting work with Socony Vacuum was to endeavour to save enough out of my salary to pay for the bridegroom's half of wedding expenses. So, on 30 June 1956, we were married by the retired Bishop of the Diocese in the small Norman church in Littlehampton in Sussex. We flew to Guernsey for our honeymoon and by the time I resumed work I had £10 left to my name! Our wedding was special. In addition to family, Una's and my friends included Peter McAlister and Peter Tetley, our cox in the Emmanuel 1st May Boat. Malcolm Tuddenham, who had played with me in the School First Eleven, was my best man. Among the telegrams was one from the Emmanuel Boat Club '10 to take her home!' – the cox's rallying call to his crew towards the last yards of a winning race – most apt – and the source of the title of my story.

At that point my trainee course had switched to do work in the Southern Industrial Marketing Office in Soho Square, London, following a similar period in the Retail Marketing Office in Sheffield. So Una and I acquired our first home – the first floor of a private house in Arnos Grove in North London which enabled her to continue her work as private secretary to the Head of the Friends Education Council in Euston. We felt a need for transport to enable us to visit Una's parents on the south coast and my father in Surrey, and we bought a Vespa scooter. At over one hundred miles to the gallon, which then cost about five shillings, it was the most economical form of transport I have ever owned! Mobil, as Socony Vacuum was by then called, moved us to the Birmingham Industrial Office where I worked as a marketing assistant. Una secured an excellent job as personal secretary to the Personnel Director of Hardy Spicer Limited – then the UK's biggest manufacturer of prop shafts for the automotive industry, with offices at Erdington. She was often chauffeur-driven to her office and earning well in excess of my then salary, so it enabled us to save up for the time when we hoped we might be able to buy a home. That moment arrived when I was appointed as an Industrial Fuels Sales Representative based in Leicester, covering a territory which included the East Midlands, Derbyshire, Lincolnshire, Northamptonshire and Warwickshire. I was to be one of a new nine-man sales force in the UK whose task was to sell the industrial fuels output from the now functioning refinery at Coryton in Essex. I took over a number of accounts from Douglas Dickie who, with his wife Dorothy, became great family friends and gave enormous support to both of us in our new existence together.

It was a case of business at the sharp end, trying to persuade commercial fleet operators and industrial companies to take Mobil fuels and lubricants. I learned a great deal about basic business relationships in the six years during which I carried out that job. At that time I used to call on industrial companies in the nether regions of Derbyshire – places like Overseal and Donisthorpe – which then looked more like the moon's landscape. Most of those companies manufactured glazed pipeclay products such as drainpipes, underground drain sections, sanitaryware and the like. My task was to try to sell Mobil products to them: fuel to fire the kilns and specialist oils to line the moulds and allow clean undamaged release of the finished product after firing was complete. Only years later was I to discover that a young Irish industrial engineer, by name Tony O'Reilly, was at the same time tramping the same unforgettable landscape working with some of the same companies. Our paths were to cross about ten years later in 1968 – of that first meeting more later.

Our move to Leicester gave Una and me our first opportunity to buy our own home. Our savings from her work at Hardy Spicer and earlier in London meant that we could afford to take out a mortgage on a small new semi-detached house in Oadby, near Leicester. We paid £2,500 plus £100 for a detached concrete garage. It is interesting to me that our mortgage repayments were about 25 per cent of my salary and our total mortgage was just over three times my annual salary, low proportions when compared to current practice.

In November 1959 our daughter Fiona was born. It was memorable not only as our first child but also because Una was having difficulty with a long labour. Our then GP, Doctor Sullivan, was hoping for a home delivery to add to his required number of home births and Olive Pearsons, our superb midwife, was doing her best to help Una meet that goal. After continued lack of success Doctor Sullivan decided reluctantly that Una must go to hospital to complete the job. The ambulance arrived and off we went, bell

Una and RDF with Ruairidh, John and Jean Rodger's boxer, Gunnislake, Cornwall, 1958

ringing in the morning rush hour. I followed by car, which was hazardous as the ambulance had to drive on the wrong side of London Road to make progress and I had to follow as I did not know where Leicester Royal Infirmary was in the city. However all went well – virtually in the lift on the way up to the maternity ward – and Fiona Susan was safely delivered at just under six pounds: a fine wee bairn.

Like most young men, I was becoming impatient at what to me seemed to be lack of progress both in terms of my responsibilities and also in my salary – which seemed to rise only by £50 increments every twelve months! So, in 1960, I started to 'look around' at other opportunities. Una persuaded me to answer an advertisement in the *Daily Telegraph* for an unknown company called McKinsey – described as a Management Consultancy. The opportunity was to join a small team of consultants in a newly-established London office – the first outside North America at that time. I arrived at the modest offices in King Street, St James', for my initial interview with Hugh Parker, the office manager. I was met by George Norfolk a retired rear admiral who was then in charge of recruiting. I remain in his debt to this day as George gave me strong advice that if questioned about my expectations for salary I should increase them by at least £500 above the number that I mentioned to him.

In the course of five subsequent interviews over the next six months I met Lee Walton, the other partner with Hugh Parker in the office at that time, and several of the then nine Associates. We all seemed to be of Oxbridge extraction and all had had different degrees of business experience. As I recall there were only two MBAs among us. After clearing the psychological interviews with Dr Sid Cabot, which was a quite unique experience never to be repeated, I was invited to join the 'Firm' and so started an eighteen year career of enormous excitement with what was to become the world's leading top Management Consultancy.

CHAPTER 7

I Survived McKinsey! (A favourite lapel badge)

IN THE LATE 1950S THE FIRM had carried out a number of major engagements for Shell Oil in Venezuela and also at Shell's London Headquarters. Both Hugh Parker and Lee Walton had been among the partners leading the study teams. This work secured a considerable amount of publicity for the Firm and at the same time the Dutch State Airline – KLM – had engaged the Firm to conduct a review of its top management organisation. These two clients provided the critical mass of work in the United Kingdom and Continental Europe to persuade the Firm's Directors in New York to decide to open the first office outside North America. London was chosen and recruitment of UK consulting staff got under way. At the time I joined the Firm in mid 1961, Allan Stewart, John Burton, Charles Bystram and Rodney Shirley were already there as Associates. An American, Sid Wilson from the Cleveland Office, was hard at work developing a planning system for Massey Ferguson UK, so he added a North American influence to the small number of British Associates. At that time the Firm's total size was of the order of about two hundred consulting staff with the major office being New York, with other US offices in Chicago, Los Angeles, San Francisco and Cleveland and, in Canada, Toronto.

In those early days of 'Start-Up' there was intense interest amongst us as to the existence of new enquiries or clients and whether studies and new clients would materialise from such enquiries. There was continuous concern as to whether there would be a sufficient study workload to give the office a base for growth in the UK. Not all clients then were major multi-national corporations. My first study was an engagement for Leonard Stace, a small producer of coated release papers and vinyl coverings based in Cheltenham. Hugh Parker directed my work as the sole Associate on a strategy review of its business. I recall that our fee for six weeks' work was £2,500 – possibly reflecting the value of my contribution as a virtually untrained consultant as well as providing the opportunity to serve a new UK client. Nevertheless I saw what were to me several growth opportunities, in particular niche areas where Stace's margins were attractive. These and other ideas seemed to go down well with the client, as well as with Hugh Parker. The preparation of that report made me realise that I had an awful lot to learn about McKinsey communication skills – one of its great strengths, skills that once learned remain with me to this day.

The real drive, focus and leadership that developed McKinsey & Company into the world's leading top Management Consultancy from its early roots as a modest accounting firm under James O. McKinsey based in Chicago and latterly in Boston, was Marvin Bower. It was Marvin who conceived and developed the notion of a firm that could provide advice to senior executives and top management based on the standards of a professional firm drawn largely from the values of the legal profession. Marvin's gospel, which he imparted to every Associate in the Firm with unstinting dedication, was based on a set of guiding principles that related to the serving of clients, the building of the Firm and being a member of its professional staff. By serving clients Marvin focused on adhering to professional standards following the top management approach, by which he meant developing relationships at the top of clients' organisations to provide leverage in assisting the client in implementation and building a capability to take up and get value out of recommendations delivered. Finally, consulting should be conducted in a cost-effective manner – in other words avoiding the accusations so often made against Management Consultants that their prime purpose is always to leave behind them an opportunity for further work.

Marvin's concern about building the Firm focused on operating as one organisation, maintaining meritocracy or a flat organisation structure and showing a genuine concern for all the Firm's people. Consistent with that philosophy was the fostering of an open and non-hierarchical working atmosphere, and finally – and sensibly – managing the Firm's resources responsibly. In other words, prudent control of costs and sensible use of the Firm's personnel resources.

Marvin really raised Management Consultancy from the realms of hack ridden charlatans concerned only with taking fees off clients to a concern that, as a member of a profession, you should demonstrate a commitment to serving clients, strive continuously for superior quality in the work done, advance the state of the art of management, and contribute to a spirit of partnership or team work and collaboration between individual consultants and offices. Most important was to profit from the freedom offered to individual consultants and to assume the responsibility associated with self-governance, which was largely the way that McKinsey's internal operations worked. Finally, and perhaps most important of all, to uphold the obligation to dissent where genuine, but different, views are held. In other words, not to be reluctant to come forward at whatever level in the Firm if you see actions or recommendations or work done that don't match standards and which you believe are not going to be effective and deliver real benefit to the client.

In the early 1960s and on into the 1980s, McKinsey used to hold an Annual Conference attended by all its consulting staff, which therefore included Directors, Principals and Associates from all its offices. These meetings offered excellent opportunities to meet and get to know all Firm members and develop an understanding of the skills they brought to bear and the nature of their client work. This knowledge was invaluable as a source of reference for help with problems or experience that could be helpful in one's own client work. As Brits from the London Office we were a relatively new phenomenon and, as is the American way, our nametags reflected the inevitable contraction of Christian names. So it was that Allan Stewart became Al Stewart, Charles Bystram became Chuck and so on. My own Christian name withstood such efforts.

In fall 1961, I attended my first Firm conference at the Westchester Country Club in the town of Westchester in Upper New York State. It was an exciting experience. My first flight in a Boeing 707 jet, my first of countless trips to the United States, it was also to be my first meeting with my US colleagues in the North American offices. We flew by day and checked into the Roosevelt Hotel in mid town Manhattan near Grand Central Station. In those days hotel rooms were shared. So John Burton and I prepared to settle down for the night knowing that we had to catch an early train the following morning from Grand Central Station to Westchester to sign in for the mid-morning start of the Conference.

You can tell how gauche and inexperienced at American habits we all were then. John, quite naturally, put his shoes outside the door in the corridor to get them cleaned overnight. Morning arrived, we re-packed and were ready to leave the room. John opened the outside door to the corridor expecting to find a pair of polished shoes ready. There were no shoes. A call to the concierge was greeted with incredulity on his part, with words to the effect of 'How dumb can you be?' After a quick financial deal with a porter who had about the same size shoes as John, we both caught the train with only minutes to spare.

I had met Marvin Bower for the first time in London shortly after I joined the firm in July 1961. Then I had been impressed – if not a little overawed – by the directness of his questions about my reasons for joining the Firm and my career hopes within it. Despite being told that I should address Marvin Bower as Marvin and not Mr Bower, coming from a British management environment where Christian names were reserved for either close friends or equally close peer colleagues, I found it difficult to start with; but it soon became the norm – and much the better for it, incidentally. During Marvin's visit to the London office, consultants and their wives were invited to a dinner to meet Marvin. Una was then heavily pregnant with our second child, our elder son Rory, who was to arrive three weeks later. John Burton, then a bachelor who sat next to her at dinner, was I think a little unnerved at Una's answer to his enquiry as to possible arrival dates.

The room-sharing arrangements continued at the Westchester Conference. Imagine my consternation when I realised that my room-mate was Marvin. To me this was the equivalent of sharing a hotel room with John Gridley, then Chairman of Mobil Oil Company in the UK! I was intrigued then at how Marvin felt the pulse and mood of the two-day Conference and translated this skill into his closing address to the assembled Firm. Again he emphasised our need to apply the professional approach to our work and the need to maintain the Firm's values of integrity, confidentiality and team work – along with the independence of mind and the ability to be forthright but supportive of colleagues and client interests.

My peers and I owe a great debt to Marvin. In our time he was the Firm and the disciplines and values that he imparted to us stayed with us and were reflected in how we tried to deliver quality solutions to clients' problems and develop and train newly joined staff. These values were still cherished by me and many of my old colleagues in our later careers – many beyond the Firm.

There was great elation in the London office when Hugh Parker announced that, after initial discussions he had had with Sir Paul Chambers, then Chairman of ICI and then one of the UK's biggest companies, Sir Paul had decided to engage the Firm to carry out a major organisation study. In my view this event marked the acceptance of McKinsey by the broad base of the British management community. New clients flowed in and the office continued to grow in size, in the increased number of consultants as well as in the vital support staff of secretaries, visual aid specialists and editors.

In the first half of the 1960s a significant part of the Firm's client work in the UK had stemmed from US based clients with operations in the United Kingdom. I have already mentioned Massey Ferguson. Another significant client relationship was with the H. J. Heinz Company in Pittsburgh, Pennsylvania. In 1960 Andy Pearson, then a New York Principal soon to become a Director of the Firm and latterly Chief Operating Officer of PepsiCo until his retirement some years ago, was directing a study with the USA Division of Heinz. This work focused on sales force effectiveness and the then new concept of product management. This was a form of organisation within consumer packaged goods companies designed to focus responsibility for a cohesive group of products into the hands of one executive able to control all those facets that affected its market position, sales revenues, cost structure and return on investment. With Pearson's help Heinz UK had adopted this structure and had appointed three of its most talented managers to the new position of Product General Manager (PGM). John Connell gave up the job of Financial Controller of the British company to become PGM in charge of soups and pasta products in which position he contributed greatly to Heinz UK's success in the mid 1960s.

This was a period of great success and growth for the British Heinz Company. It opened a major new canning and bottling plant at Kit Green near Wigan in Lancashire, and was among the first UK consumer packaged goods companies to institute major national sales/marketing promotions along with major trade incentives. They were the years of 57 Mini-Minor cars and 57 holiday promotions – which had massive impact in the grocery trade and on consumers at that time.

With John Lutz, who was on a two-year transfer from the New York office, I was the other Associate implementing a major programme of sales force reorganisation, working with Heinz UK executives. The increasing spread of the new multiples such as Tesco and Sainsbury and the development of wholesale buying groups such as Spar and Macro meant that the days of large national sales forces calling on virtually all shops and trying to sell direct to store owners were becoming both uneconomical and counter-productive. Even then the number of small grocery stores in the UK was in sharp decline. In this fast changing consumer and trading environment the key was to develop the skills needed to sell marketing programmes to multiple head office buyers and use a reorganised sales force to follow up at store level to help implement such promotions by checking that agreed shelving, shelf prices and merchandising materials were in position and on display. Similarly these new selling approaches were needed to deal successfully with the number of increasingly powerful wholesalers where the job of assisting their sales people was becoming increasingly important and necessary to generate full co-operation and to maximise sales at retail level.

So for the consumer packaged goods marketer new skills were needed. Key Account selling or what we at McKinsey came to develop as Trade Marketing called for skills far removed from traditional field sales management. Eight hundred sales representatives calling on over eighty thousand outlets were no longer needed to cover the 80 per cent of all commodity volume. That was then the target for most national manufacturers.

Today in the UK four major multiple accounts deliver over 75 per cent of the sales volume for most national consumer packaged goods manufacturers. That process of concentration was already getting under way in the mid 1960s. So McKinsey's work with Heinz UK was ground breaking at the time. Two pilot sales branches were set up and Key Account management was formally constituted. We were reasonably popular with the Heinz sales people as this work brought forward the provision of company cars for field sales personnel. No longer did a bowler hatted salesman have to travel by bus armed with a sample bag and the day's supply of display material.

It had become customary at Firm Annual Conferences for some entertainment to be offered. In the 1960s the satirical show *Beyond The Fringe* had developed a strong following in the USA. It was suggested that the London Office should try to emulate this trend at the next conference. John Maley had had experience in an RAF

Radio service in Cyprus during his national service, so he put a set of verses together to be sung by a quartet of London associates. So, in the Tarrytown Inn in Poughkeepsie, New York, we launched into our piece. Our reprise was 'London keep your pecker up!' We had expected some audience response but at the first reprise there was a dead, almost embarrassed, silence and the same during the second. By the time we reached the third the roof came in. Our US colleagues had realised that we Brits had absolutely no idea of the American connotation of the phrase! Similarly I have since described this difference in language between us as 'In the USA I wear my vest and pants on the outside whereas in the UK, I wear those garments on the inside!'

My next study was to provide me with my first experience of work and travel in the USA. John Flint, an American partner then in the London Office, asked me to work with him on an examination of the USA market for radioactively labelled chemical compounds used in medical research and diagnostic medicine. Our client was to be the Radiochemical Centre at Amersham, subsequently to become Amersham International. An offshoot from the British Atomic Energy Authority at Harwell, it had established a leadership position in this specialised field. Its main market outside the UK was the USA. Stewart Burgess, then a Scientific Officer at the Centre and ultimately to become Amersham's CEO, was seconded to our team to provide expert technical and product knowledge.

Despite its strong position the Centre used an agent in the USA so had little or no knowledge of the identity and product application characteristics of its customers who were mostly research institutions, major hospitals and universities. Our task was to make direct contact with a wide sample of these customers to better understand their needs and use for the Centre's products as an input to a new strategy for increased market penetration, including possible establishment of a direct selling organisation in the USA.

Based in the New York Office we were joined by John Stewart, then an Associate based in the office, and for part of the six-week work in the US by Bob Worcester from the Washington DC office who has since become founding Chairman of MORI, the UK polling organisation. Interviewing customers from coast to coast such as the National Institutes of Health in Washington DC, Mount Sinai Hospital in New York and UCLA on the west coast we quickly realised that significant market share had been lost and the solution was to go with technical support direct from the UK. I enjoyed the added experience of travel to new places and learned the art of using a Bell Telephone credit card and a 25-cent piece in a pay-phone for telephone interviews across the US. It also gave me my first experience of driving on the right-hand side of the road when I rented a Ford Galaxy in mid town Manhattan to drive to Princeton, New Jersey via the Lincoln Tubes, to meet research personnel at the university there. During this study I also visited Harvard and was able to see on the plinth supporting the statue of John Harvard in Harvard Square the crest of Emmanuel College, Cambridge whence John Harvard had graduated and moved to Cambridge, Massachusetts where he later died and left his library as a foundation for a seat of learning there to become one the world's leading centres of academic excellence.

In 1965 Winston Churchill died. It was almost as though a revered elderly relative had passed away. To this day, I can recall the tone of his voice as he made his magnificent wartime speeches. He lay in state in Westminster Hall close by the House of Commons. One evening during the period of his lying-in-state I had to stay overnight at the Carlton Tower Hotel off Sloane Street. I had undressed and was lying in bed when suddenly I thought I must go and witness this event and pay my respects. So I got up, dressed, and made my way to Westminster to join the thousands waiting in line. I joined the line at 11.00 p.m. on the other side of the Thames River opposite Big Ben. The atmosphere was incredible and so like wartime. Tea wagons were providing hot drinks; all around me others were chatting with each other, many reminiscing about wartime experiences and many from abroad. At 4.00 a.m., I finally entered the great hall, descended down the stone steps and filed past the catafalque. So I returned to my hotel room well satisfied and able to give a first hand account to Una and my children and, more recently, to my grandchildren.

Another milestone in the development of the London Office practice was reached when the Firm was engaged by Shell and BP to address the issue of whether, and if so how, Shell Mex and BP (SMBP) should be broken up and its respective parts linked back to the individual parent oil companies. SMBP was then the distributing, marketing and sales organisation owned jointly by Shell and BP. It had the major market share in every sector of oil and lubricant consumption in the UK – from retail to industrial and to commercial fuels and lubricants. Only in crude oil trading, refining and aviation sales, did each parent operate independently in the UK and compete with each other. Esso was SMBP's major competitor in the UK, with Regent and Mobil and a number of other small companies a long way behind with relatively small market shares. While dominant and successful, SMBP stood in the way of each parent company building its own brand identity and position in its home market, as well as in some cases restricting exploitation in the UK of each company's new products or other innovative strategies for fear of loss of initiative to the other company.

John Davies (originally a BP man) was the then Managing Director of SMBP. John Birkin and Tom Grieve were Shell representatives on the SMBP Board and Chris Laidlaw was one of two BP representatives. We assembled a sizable study team for this work. The study was directed by Lee Walton and John McDonald, a bluff Yorkshireman who had joined the Firm in New York from Raytheon and was to build the firm's impressive practice in Germany in the 1970s and 1980s. I was put on the team, no doubt given my Mobil work experience and sales management work at Heinz.

At the conclusion of the diagnostic phase we delivered our recommendations to the Shell and BP representatives. The recommendations were designed to start the process of separation, firstly in coverage of the retail market. After discussion our recommendations were finally accepted, albeit with some reluctance, by John Davies. I was to be part of a joint SMBP and McKinsey team, designing and implementing a new sales organisation for the industrial and commercial market. Bob Ingle and John Riddell-Webster were to be my team mates. We had a great deal of fun as well as serious work as we took our Roadshow round the SMBP divisions across the UK. There were serious issues to be addressed as, at that time, SMBP was organised into geographic Divisions with a powerful Divisional Manager charged with full responsibility for nearly all sales within his Division. The effect of the implementation of the McKinsey recommendations was to start to dismantle this structure and replace it with national structures organised around business/product groupings where line accountability was held at the national level. It was in fact the classic issue for most large organisations, whether they were national or international, namely geographic versus product accountability.

This organisational dilemma was succinctly, and impishly characterised in a short ditty by Leslie Miles given to me by Bill Hamm of
Continental Oil in 1966 that I keep to this day.

REORGANISATION
Here we go round the mulberry bush . . .
Efficiency and economy require over-all control –
Centralize. Centralize.
The top mustn't do what can be done below –
Decentralize, Decentralize.
Authority should be vested in divisional boards –
Centralize, Centralize.
Staff respond best to a personal boss –
Decentralize, Decentralize.
Functions in common must be grouped and axed –
Centralize, Centralize.
Accountability develops responsible men –
Decentralize, Decentralize.
Here we go round the mulberry bush on a cold and frosty morning.

Another team with Christopher Saunders as the McKinsey
member was tasked with designing a new approach and strategy for
the domestic home heating market, which also included SMBP
Distributors.

At that time, Lee Walton was also Managing Director of
McKinsey's Chicago Office, then with a staff of about forty
Consultants. He had been deeply involved in the SMBP study in
particular given his previous working relationships with Birkin and
Grieve in the earlier Shell studies. On one occasion after a
presentation early in 1965, returning in a cab from Shell Mex House
in the Strand to our offices in King Street, Lee told me that Shell had
asked him whether they could approach me to join them and work
on similar implementation work in their other major companies
outside the UK. After this modest flattery, Lee followed up with a
suggestion that instead, I should consider becoming the first Brit to
be exported in reverse back to the USA by accepting a transfer to the
Chicago Office.

Una and I had just exchanged contracts on the purchase of an
attractive larger house on high ground overlooking Dorking, where
we had lived since coming south from the Midlands when I joined
the Firm. By then Una's parents and my father were well into their

70s and our two children, Fiona at 6 and Rory at 4, were happily established at their primary and nursery schools nearby. It seemed however like too good an experience and opportunity to pass up from both a career and a family development viewpoint. So, in October 1965, some two or three months after we had moved into our new home in Dorking, we locked it up, placed McNibbs, our four-year old boxer dog, with a nearby farmer, and booked our TWA flight from Heathrow to Chicago. Delayed for six hours we shared the small first-class TWA lounge with Joan Collins – even then a well-known actress and star.

We arrived at O'Hare Airport outside Chicago to be met by Tal Honey, the Administrative Manager at the Chicago Office. He drove us all to the Orrington Hotel in Evanston, which was to be our home for the four to six weeks it took us to find a suitable apartment. Lois, Lee Walton's wife, arrived shortly afterwards at the Orrington to add her warmth to our welcome – which at the time was very much appreciated.

Before leaving London we had been assured by Chicago that we could rent furniture, find an apartment and secure school places for the children with little or no trouble after our arrival. Unfortunately we were to learn quickly that in the United States schools resume after Labour Day in early September and, as a consequence, the most attractive options for apartment choices had already been taken. In addition furniture could not be rented and good school places were already filled. Nevertheless we found an attractive fourteenth floor three-bedroom apartment in East Chestnut Street in downtown Chicago – in fact where the Hancock Building now stands. We purchased the necessary furniture, bedding etc. and commenced our first experience of living and working in the USA.

Fiona had attended an excellent small church school at Dorking. The first Chicago school we visited had two thousand pupils, and was in a less desirable part of Chicago with a minority of white pupils. Fiona would have been overwhelmed. So with help from Tom Reeves, a partner in the office, a place was found for Fiona at the Latin School in the city – an excellent private school. Rory was accepted at the North Shore Country Day School in Evanston on the outskirts of Chicago, run by a Mr and Mrs Rich. It was about a twenty-five minute drive up Lakeshore Drive so a car was needed. After a search we decided on a Ford Mustang – Lee Iacocca's cult car launched in 1964.

Buying a car in the United States was to experience serious solicitation and service at its best in contrast to its then UK equivalent. Seated in a dealer's warm, comfortable office in November we selected colour, interior finish, extra items like undersealing etc. Our selections made, I was driven to a vast snow-covered parking lot nearby. Stopping at a particular snow-covered vehicle the salesman wiped off the snow on the wing to check colour. Within ninety minutes with a loan arranged for the price of 2,800 US dollars, we drove away as proud owners. I call that service and even after the purchase I was still receiving calls from other dealers eager to get my business or cut the price even further.

As was typical of life in McKinsey my first study was for the Continental Oil Company whose offices were in New York, Houston and Los Angeles. Directed by Lee Walton with me as the engagement manager, the study involved almost continuous weekly commuting between New York, Houston and Los Angeles leaving Una to set up home in our new apartment. Continental Oil was then a fully integrated oil company run by Leonard F. McCullum, a colourful Texan, notable for keeping his telephone in the lower right-hand drawer of his desk and occasionally using a spittoon with great accuracy sited in the far corner of his New York office. He would also hold his management meetings sitting at the head of a board table surrounded by squawk boxes, thus avoiding extensive travel to the outposts of his empire. Continental had recently merged with Consolidation Coal as part of its strategy to become a broader energy based business. Continental's pipeline company was run out of Oklahoma City, Tennessee, by Bill Kyger, a sun-wizened gent from Tennessee. He and I became good friends but not until he was able to understand my British accent and in turn I was able to disentangle his deep southern accent, not helped by a cleft palate. Their US domestic headquarters was in Houston, Texas, under Bill Hamm, a good oil man and a very fine manager. On one occasion I had to fly from Houston to New York with Continental's chief legal counsel who was due to make an appearance in a Court in New York at 10 a.m. the next day. It was mid December and by the time we neared New York a snowstorm was raging. After circling and having made an aborted landing over La Guardia Airport our pilot flew on up to Boston, arriving there at about 11.30 p.m. We disembarked to find that all trains and buses to New York had long since departed.

With my travelling companion's need to be in New York the next morning, we rented a car. He said he would drive and I did not demur – after all he was the client. So we headed off along the expressway towards New York. The road was atrocious with deep slush on the surface, snow falling and large trucks throwing up water and more slush at us as they passed by.

After two 360° skids I enquired how comfortable with driving conditions was my companion? He replied, 'I haven't driven up here for over twenty-five years.' I suggested I should take over. After a further two hours driving we were somewhere in north Connecticut. My companion vouchsafed that 'I used to live around here so let's go off the highway and pick up the mail train into New York. It will save time and should be an easy ride.' My second mistake, after letting him drive in the first place, was to follow his advice. Needless to say he lost our way so I pulled up outside a gas station to get directions back to the expressway. As I was talking to the gas station attendant on the forecourt, around the corner came a snow plough. It passed our parked car and nearly buried it under snow. The attendant kindly lent us shovels and the three of us dug the car out and, with his instructions, found the expressway and finally reached New York at about 9.30 a.m. My companion just made his Court appearance and I arrived in the New York office, then in the Union Carbide building on Park Avenue, somewhat exhausted but ready to continue the task of writing the Firm's report to Continental management. For those readers who have seen Steve Martin and John Candy in the film *Planes, Trains and Automobiles*, this incident will have a familiar ring to it!

For some reason I had found this work difficult and time-consuming despite – or perhaps because of – the help from the McKinsey editors in New York. While checking over the final hundred-page draft in my 32nd floor office that looked over to the Chemical Bank building across Park Avenue, I was suddenly transfixed. A complete sheet glass window panel in the wall of the office opposite detached itself from its frame and descended like a falling leaf to shatter like a spilled bucket of water into a hundred fragments on the sidewalk below. Luckily no pedestrians were hit or hurt. However, in coming away the glass panel created a vacuum so that the contents of the man's office opposite were also fluttering down after the glass, despite his frantic efforts to claw back some of what were no doubt vital papers. For a moment I contemplated how I would have addressed the same problem if I had lost my final draft in the same way. I think I might have jumped after it!

My next study was with Western Publishing, a fascinating publishing business based in Racine, Wisconsin. Western had very close relationships with the Disney organisation and owned publishing rights to a number of Disney characters and story books. One of its subsidiaries, Artists and Writers, provided much of the drawing and design skill for the books published by Western. These were amongst the most creative and interesting people that I met during my time at McKinsey.

My final study in the Chicago office was for General Mills. The task was to evaluate the attractiveness to General Mills of acquiring the Playskool Company, the children's toy and learning business based in New York. An unusual product line – the envy of most children – Playskool had found itself with one of its products named 'The Toy of the Year'. Demand for the 'Tike Bike' went through the roof. Management displaced production of other lines as well as contracting to third parties plants to meet demand. To Playskool's surprise and disappointment they achieved record sales revenues, selling over one million Tike Bikes, but achieved only marginal profits. Their pricing judgement and systems had let them down badly. For example an increase of one dollar at retail would have taken one million dollars to the bottom line, with probably little or no damage to sales. Sloppy costing systems and the use of accrual accounting had trapped them: a lesson that I took with me forever afterwards.

On 4 January 1967, Una, I and the children sailed from New York on the SS *United States* bound for Southampton. It was a very rough crossing. On arrival, by pre-arrangement, the AA adjusted the lights on our Mustang and we drove home. But not before Rory, then six years old, asked me a searching question as we stood on the dockside at Southampton. 'Daddy,' he asked, 'why don't the policemen here wear guns?' An unusual question but perhaps a reflection of the calmer times in which the UK was able to live in those years, sadly far removed from the much more violent society that pervades the country today.

CHAPTER 8

Practice Building

IN JULY 1967 I WAS ELECTED a Principal or Junior Partner in the Firm. In addition to having my own office and choosing its furnishing, more importantly, I started to think more about what sort of contribution I could make to the Firm and to the further development of my own career. I had become increasingly interested in the work that I had done in marketing and sales, and at the same time had become concerned that we were lacking in real consumer marketing experience amongst our consulting staff, who at that point were comprised largely of generalists. One of the great strengths of McKinsey was the opportunity it offered to the individual Associate or Partner to define an area that he or she wanted to develop that would generate client work and broaden the Firm's understanding or its reputation in particular areas of practice. Obviously opening new offices was major amongst those opportunities but there was also an increasing need to develop more specialised skills in certain areas of our practice.

In the early 1960s in the USA Andy Pearson, under the auspices of General Foods, had carried out a series of industry-wide studies developing the concept of Direct Product Profitability. At its simplest his notion was that to be able to identify the costs incurred at each stage as a product moved through the system from procurement, production, distribution to marketing and finally to sales off the retail shelf, would lead to a better understanding of the relative profit contribution derived from the sales of one product group versus another when related to its velocity or number of units sold in a given period. Obviously this would provide a valuable tool in addressing the profitability of new products as well as existing lines and in identifying opportunities to lower costs and improve contribution or, conversely, to delete lines where economical to do so. This work generated considerable interest in the consumer package goods community in the United States and had achieved some notice in the UK. Indeed the PGM work done at Heinz was in part the embodiment of the same concept. A small group of Consultants recruited from US consumer package goods companies had over time assembled in US offices. It seemed to me that we had similar needs in the UK if we were to gain greater credibility and, therefore, effectiveness in work with British consumer goods companies.

So, with the agreement of my other London partners, we set about hiring a small number of Associates who could bring tried and tested experience to our studies in the areas of marketing strategy, sales promotion and advertising, and product management, and who had potential to succeed in the Firm. We developed a first-class team, including Peter Foy from Gillette, Norman Sanson, Richard Norton, John Banham, now Sir John Banham, John Beard and Bruce Noble. This group was augmented by continuing recruitment in ensuing years.

We also established a dedicated research capability and hired Hilary Peart, tasked to collate our study work and maintain and develop contacts with leading research organisations in the industry to avoid re-inventing the wheel when similar information was needed on different studies. Her work was also valuable as a training and induction aid for newly joined Associates. While it was vital to nurture the creative ability of consultants' problem-solving skills, this

'And the second issue we must resolve is . . .!' Problem solving in my office at
McKinsey & Company, 74 St James's Street, London SW1, 1974

support also enabled more effort to be directed to team brainstorming for relevant – even radical – solutions that would really deliver benefit to the client.

I believed strongly – and still do – that such benefit was not embodied in a revised or new organisation chart or a new job specification. These had their place, but it seemed to me that the real test of the Firm's contribution was to have been seen to help management deliver improved performance (by which I mean an increase in market share, improved advertising spend efficiency, etc.) that translated into improved margins, higher return on investment, more solid cash flow and a stronger balance sheet.

Therefore the 'best' clients, and those who were usually the most stimulating and exciting to work with, were those senior executives who challenged us vigorously and joined with us in the development of recommendations and improved strategies.

The problem-solving discipline practised by McKinsey was one of its most effective tools. At its root were really two notions. First, if you can accurately identify the key issue(s) underlying the problem, their resolution will probably provide beneficial courses of action able to solve the problem and deliver benefit. To achieve that result it is then necessary to develop hypotheses that, when developed and tested by analysis, will prove or disprove that those courses of action will resolve the key issue and are both feasible and actionable. The second notion, equally important, was to rely on facts and rigorous analysis of them. Facts are friendly and successful strategy is so often the result of a deep understanding of the issues and possible alternative courses of action arrived at by thorough analysis. Logic obviously also has its place in this process.

Sound management judgement and experience also play their own vital part in the problem-solving process. In my view there are still situations where, despite exhaustive research and analysis that indicate a particular course of action, mature judgement – or gut feel – tells you that it's not the right solution. And your gut feel can still be the right course of action to follow.

The Consumer Group, as this team came to be known, trail blazed and was in time followed by the establishment of similar Interest Groups in banking and financial services, developing countries practice, etc. The nurturing of these Interest Groups also allowed for a more sensible exchange of consulting skills between groups and in due course between offices, which allowed new perspectives to be brought to bear in the solution of problems.

In my time the Consumer Group made a valuable contribution to the London office and at times provided a disproportionate share of the client workload there. Virtually all of its founder members went on to enjoy leadership positions in industry and in the higher echelons of McKinsey. Our client base grew and included many leading players in the UK consumer packaged goods industry.

In the late 1960s I responded to a request from Tesco, the UK supermarket chain, to meet the Board to discuss a possible study of their organisation and strategy. That meeting was memorable. It was my first encounter with Sir John Cohen, better known as Jack Cohen, Tesco's founder. He was obviously rightly proud of a business that had pioneered the introduction of self-service retailing into the United Kingdom under the slogan 'pile it high and sell it cheap'. But times were changing in the 1960s and early 70s. Supermarkets with their greater space, product assortment and car parking facilities were starting to overtake the small self-service store of about 2,500 square feet with its narrow crowded aisles, inevitable congestion for customers and limited product assortment. Many of these stores were badly located in high streets. At that time they constituted a very significant part of Tesco's 600 to 700 stores.

Jack was then in his late seventies and still dangerously dominant in the company's operations, despite having theoretically handed over much of the day-to-day operating responsibility to others.

At that meeting he presented me with two mementoes that I still have. The first was a long playing record entitled 'Tesco', in which Jack discussed how he and his friends started the business and built it up from its origins when, as a World War I demobilised veteran, he started selling army surplus 'stuff' off his barrow in East London. The second item that he gave me was a tie clip with the letters 'YCDBSOYA' carved on the bar. As he handed over the tie clip he said, 'These letters describe my business philosophy – You Can't Do Business Sitting On Your Ass!' At its most basic this is, I suppose, not a bad guideline for future success!

We were asked to submit proposals for the work that Tesco wanted to have carried out. Negotiating that study was equally memorable. In my first meeting, Jack had described with much satisfaction how he had bargained with a well-known City investment bank to reduce

their fees for a particular assignment, so when I proposed that we
conduct a three to four month diagnostic analysis of their business at
a fee of £X, Jack queried as to why we couldn't complete that phase
in two months at half £X. At that point, one of Jack's colleagues,
Arthur Thrush, did chide him with, 'Come on, Jack, hiring
McKinsey is not the same as getting a lower price on an order for
Heinz baked beans!'

Satisfactory terms were agreed and our study got under way. Tesco
then operated about 600–700 stores in England. They had no
representation in Scotland. Store operations and distribution were
organised into Tesco North and Tesco South. These divisions were
run by two younger upcoming managers. Ron Bronstein, Managing
Director, Tesco North, located at Winsford, Cheshire; and Ian
MacLaurin, Managing Director, Tesco South, located at Cheshunt,
the company's Headquarters in Hertfordshire.

One of several issues of concern was how to raise the profitability
of individual stores up to the level of the best. The team set up an
exhaustive analysis of every element that was likely to correlate with
both high and low profitability in each store. These elements
included, for example, site location, floor area of the store, number
of product categories carried and the ranges within those categories,
the number of employees by department, and the gross margin mix
– depending on space allocation between dry groceries, meat and
butchered products, non-foods, and finally the age and length of
service of the store manager. The results of this detailed analysis were
revealing. The dominant variable that had the greatest correlation
with high profit was the length of service of the store manager
concerned. In other words, the longer the store manager had been in
position the higher the profits generated by that store tended to be.
The store manager also had significant leeway in generating ways to
increase sales. The converse also proved to be true and perhaps was
self evident. If store profits consistently missed target or declined the
manager would find himself replaced. In other words 'fired'. Put
simply: if a manager could not make money out of his store he would
be job-hunting pretty soon.

Perhaps this is a blunt instrument when viewed thirty years on but
it did focus the mind of each manager and it also focused senior
management on the need to spread best practice through training and
the development of store managers.

As the study progressed it quickly became obvious that persuading Jack to step back from the business and accept retirement gracefully was vital if Tesco was to be able to grapple successfully with its emerging competitors and also drive through the changes needed in its retail offering, along with the supporting infrastructure of financial systems and supply chain that would be needed. After careful review with individual Board members, we believed we had developed a structure that, if Jack could be persuaded to accept it, would allow a smooth transition to take place. Nevertheless I was still anxious that Jack would refuse to accept what were in effect his Board's recommendations and, if so, what the outcome might be. Given Jack's unpredictability I was also concerned that McKinsey could well become the subject of adverse publicity.

These concerns were heightened when, on the eve of our presentation to the full Board, I received a call from Hyman Kreitman, Jack's son-in-law and a long serving Board member, to meet him at his London home that evening. The plan to be put to the Board included the appointment of Jack as Life President with his own office and elevator in the new offices to be built at Cheshunt, and Hyman Kreitman was to be appointed Chairman and Chief Executive of the company.

On my arrival, Kreitman took me to his study and told me that if Jack and all the Board rejected our recommendations he was no longer prepared to soldier on and would offer his resignation from the Board and the company. He then read over to me the statement that he would make to the Board tomorrow if things did not go well.

The following day we joined the Board Meeting with all directors present and after my introduction our engagement manager, Jim Fisher, delivered our recommendations. Each director was then asked for his view. As this was proceeding with each director indicating qualified support to the new structure, suddenly Jack interrupted and delivered a verbal broadside to the effect that, as the person who had built the business and who had delivered prosperity to everyone, he would sell his stock and bring down the value of the business. The atmosphere was tense. At that moment the door to the Board Room opened and the tea lady arrived. Everyone froze and for what seemed an age the good lady served each of us with tea and biscuits and then pushed the trolley out of the room and left. I then noticed Hyman Kreitman reach into the breast pocket of his jacket. I knew what was going to happen next. He asked for silence, pulled out the paper that I had reviewed with him the previous evening and emphasised that Tesco was now a major public company and no longer a private fiefdom. He then read his statement aloud, gathered his papers and left the Board Room.

In the stunned silence that followed his departure Arthur Thrush, one of Jack Cohen's oldest associates, asked, 'What do we do now?' Laurie Don, Tesco's Finance Director, replied, 'When this meeting closes we must inform the Stock Exchange of Hyman Kreitman's resignation.'

At that point I considered that the McKinsey team members present should leave the Board and stand by to be available if needed. After waiting for an hour or more word came that we should leave and that the Board would call us as to any outcome. The following day I was informed that the Board Meeting had been adjourned – not ended – thus avoiding any need to advise the Stock Exchange as no formal decisions had been made or decided. In the next two days I received calls from two directors asking me to consider changing or modifying our recommendations to ease the impasse. In each case I replied that I felt unable to do so as I firmly believed that our recommendations properly reflected the views of the Board and were appropriate to allow the business to move forward and develop its undoubted potential.

Two more days went by and then Laurie Don called me with the news that after all, our recommendations had been accepted in full, Jack had agreed to become President and Hyman Kreitman had withdrawn his resignation and had been appointed Chairman and Chief Executive.

Tesco's subsequent story is well known and how, under the outstanding leadership of Ian, now Lord, MacLaurin, the business carried out fundamental change to become the UK's most successful retail supermarket operation, achieving and retaining the leading market share, having moved upmarket in its consumer offering and led the way in superstore development and profitability.

Looking back on that study I believe we were right to stick to our guns. The resulting changes did pave the way for what Ian MacLaurin describes so well in his book *Tiger By The Tail*.

Fixed as he was in his ways, Jack neither could, nor would, admit that he, rather than the times, should change, and in the late 1960s,

McKinseys were called in, in an attempt to resolve the impasse. I have always had my suspicions about management consultants. They are all very well when it comes to working to a deadline, but all too often they entrench themselves in the interstices of a company, and then they become the very devil to remove. I must say, however, that McKinseys didn't dawdle about reaching their conclusions, possibly because they found it impossible to unravel the shambolic situation that passed for management at Tesco House. Baffled by what they found, McKinseys coined the masterly understatement that the 'Board does not fulfil its functions in the most disciplined manner', to recommend that it should 'exercise more self discipline in interpreting its role and conducting its meetings'.

Shortly after the Tesco study I received a call from John (now Lord) Sainsbury, then Chairman of J. Sainsbury. He wanted to discuss their interest in investigating possible entry into non-foods, away from their traditional dry grocery business. This turned out to be a fascinating piece of work, requiring us to examine the prospects for growth and profitability and the economics of an array of different types of retail operation in sectors as varied as clothing, garden centres, electrical consumer electronics and white goods.

John Sainsbury was an exhilarating client to work with. Autocratic in manner, he had already achieved an enviable record in transforming his father's heritage of traditional, well respected high street grocery stores into a modern supermarket chain which at that time and for many years after was to sustain its position as the number one UK grocery retailer – only to see that position lost as Tesco during the 1980s, under Ian MacLaurin's leadership, overtook them to take and keep the number one position.

One of the reasons that led to the formation of the Consumer Interest Group in the UK and later its extension into Europe was to enable closer liaison with the work of a similar group of consultants centred in the Firm's New York office. Andy Pearson, now a director in the Firm, had led a number of studies with leading US package goods companies and Tom Wilson had joined the Firm from Proctor & Gamble where he had been a Product General Manager.

There had been much discussion and debate in the USA about the prospects of being able to develop a form of electronic coding of individual product items to take advantage of developing computer technology and thereby to provide better analysis of item movement in store and from manufacturer through to retailer and the claimed benefits that would result in improved profitability to both parties. A joint industry working group had been established to study the prospects in the United States, led by R. Burt Gookin, then Chief Executive Officer of the H. J. Heinz Company in Pittsburgh. That group had hired McKinsey to conduct the necessary analysis and Tom Wilson, supported by Larry Russell, led this work on behalf of the Firm. The Grocery Manufacturers of America (GMA) also lent its support and the Universal Product Code (UPC) as it came to be called, was developed and tested, along with extensive work with IBM to design and test a system of electronic bar coding that could be both unique to each individual product item and capable of being read by laser at a newly designed retail checkout.

Several retail pilot operations were established to test the system and the technology and to identify savings both hard and soft. Hard savings related to areas such as lower labour costs arising from the removal of the job of bagger at a re-designed checkout, virtual elimination of theft and shrinkage. Soft savings were defined as those areas such as the use of accurate data on the movement of items through the distribution system, item velocity at the checkout and the better allocation of shelf space to improve profitability – all much more difficult to measure but in the long run of greater impact on overall profitability.

I visited an A & P pilot store in Englewood, New Jersey during a visit to the New York office. Sitting beside the store manager in his office overlooking thirty checkouts, it was fascinating to watch how he could change price on an item and see it reflected immediately in the activity at each checkout. He could check cash balances at each till and had at his finger tips information on item movement. For example, by entering in a new price for a particular item on his console he could see, virtually immediately, whether lowering or raising price translated into higher or lower sales of the item.

Consumers were concerned that the removal of shelf price and in its place a bar code would lead to confusion and risk over-pricing etc. There was also concern amongst the Retail Employees Union that this would reduce labour at the checkout by leading to the elimination of the job of bagger. However, trials demonstrated conclusively that UPC would only pay off if a high enough percentage of all retailers signed up to the scheme, and that it would be administered centrally and independently with strict control over the allocation of unique codes to individual manufacturers, retailers and product. There was also concern as to whether such a system would have application beyond dry grocery products and whether expensive checkout equipment needed at that time would prove economical for slower moving non food categories. Alongside the US developments and trials Albert Heijn, the Chairman and Chief Executive of the Albert Heijn retail grocery chain in Holland, was following these developments closely and launched his own trials of the system in a selection of his stores in that country.

It seemed to me that UPC with its ability to provide both manufacturer and retailer with accurate data on the movement of individual products through the supply chain, and the generation of accurate data on consumer buying habits and the effectiveness of promotion and also of advertising, had to be the way of the future. However, an obvious snag in its development and exploitation by the industry in the UK, was the relative antipathy that existed between manufacturers and retailers, and between individual retailers who both prized confidentiality and maintained intensely competitive positions vis-à-vis each other. So the apparent need to co-operate in the development of such a system was prima facie anathema to its potential for serious success.

My initial exploratory discussions with one or two clients, particularly manufacturers, suggested that interest in the UK was a long way behind the progress already being made in the USA and to a lesser extent in Europe by Albert Heijn. The UK industry did not have then an equivalent organisation to the GMA in the USA. In the USA there were examples of co-operation such as the National Association of Food Chains which had helped UPC work move along and be developed. At that time the Institute of Grocery Distribution (IGD) was the nearest that the UK industry could offer. Then it was a relatively looseknit association of several retailers and a small number of leading manufacturers. Nevertheless I felt that it would be worth while to see whether our extensive work in helping the US industry develop UPC and set up the necessary structures to manage the system on a USA wide basis would be applicable to the UK industry's situation. Tom Wilson and I had discussions with the IGD committee and in due course were asked to present proposals to examine the feasibility and attractiveness of adopting a similar system for the UK grocery industry. Such proposals were to take account of the preliminary work done on an article numbering system in which Sainsbury's had co-operated with Albert Heijn, utilising electronic point of sale equipment (EPOS) already under test.

It was a complex piece of work as we had to be able to evaluate the point at which the costs of the installation of equipment, systems and organisation for the administration of an Article Numbering System (ANS), as it was called in the UK, would be more than offset by the hard and soft savings that could be achieved throughout the industry. It was also important to be able to demonstrate the absolute feasibility of establishing the uniqueness and therefore confidentiality of the code for each item attributable to the manufacturer and the retailer through whom the same item was finally sold to the consumer in store. This gave rise to the design of the bar code and its ten digit content which allowed a portion of the code to be unique to the manufacturer and the item, and a portion to be unique to the retailer for the same item.

Our study demonstrated that approximately 75 per cent of all commodity volume (ACV) sold through grocery retailers would need to be included in such a system for it to start to generate benefits across the industry. It would probably take two to four years at least to reach such a point and would require significant investment, particularly on the part of retailers, to install the necessary point of sale equipment and the related systems. Hard savings were relatively easy to identify in terms of better utilisation of store labour, better control over shrinkage, and cash. Soft savings, i.e. in the availability of information to understand better the flow of product profit through the system, and how better to control and monitor movement of goods and their related cost through the system, were much more difficult to quantify although certainly available.

In a sense UPC and its UK equivalent ANS were the logical developments from the direct product profit studies conducted by Andy Pearson for the National Association of Food Chains back in the early 60s, under the sponsorship of General Foods. John Phillips worked with me as the Engagement Manager on the UK work and we were able to capitalise on Tom Wilson's and Larry Russell's earlier work in the USA. Suffice to say that this study did pioneer the adoption of article numbering in the UK, which has now become the norm across virtually all types of retailing. Indeed bar coding has extended into many other fields of activity; for example, it is now widely in use in the airline industry to identify individual items of baggage as they move through or at times get lost in the carriage of bags from one point to another.

In the spring of 1969 our second son and third child arrived. James Alisdair was delivered at Crawley Hospital in Surrey after a difficult pregnancy for Una. Both Fiona and Rory had set their hearts on receiving a sister, so the reader can understand my relief and joy when the nurse came out of the operating theatre and announced that it was a girl. Then she went back into the theatre. A few seconds later she dashed out and with some embarrassment told me she had got it wrong the first time and in fact our newborn was a boy. To this day I have never understood how the mistake was made!

In 1972 I was elected a director of the Firm, some eleven years after I had joined. In addition to my interest in consumer goods work, the other area that I spent much time on was the development of the Firm's practice in the Republic of Ireland. The Bank of Ireland had been a client in the mid 60s under its leadership of Ian Morrison and Don Carroll. Don Carroll was also Chairman and Chief Executive of P J Carroll, the market leader in the Republic's cigarette market. Anton Rupert's company, Rembrandt, the South African tobacco company, held a majority stake in Carroll's business. David Griffiths, one of my partners in London, had worked closely with Morrison and Carroll in their banking operations. I became involved with Don Carroll as a result of his interest in our carrying out some work in P J Carroll. Actually we carried out several studies for Don Carroll, covering product market strategy and sales effectiveness in their marketplace in the Irish Republic.

At that time in the early 70s inflation was starting to rise fast and risking serious danger to the development of the Irish economy. Morrison and Carroll decided that a project should be undertaken to analyse, understand and communicate the causes of high and rising rates of inflation and the effect that such rises were having on company profits, cash flow and balance sheets, particularly in the areas of debt management. Such a report was to be made available widely in Ireland. The study was duly completed with major input from eminent Irish economists, in particular David Whitaker, the Chief Economist at the Bank of Ireland. It was published as the McKinsey Report. I think it did help to alert management to the erosion of value under conditions of high inflation and the need for replacement cost techniques accompanied by prompt re-valuation of inventories reflected in offsetting price increases to maintain adequate cash flow.

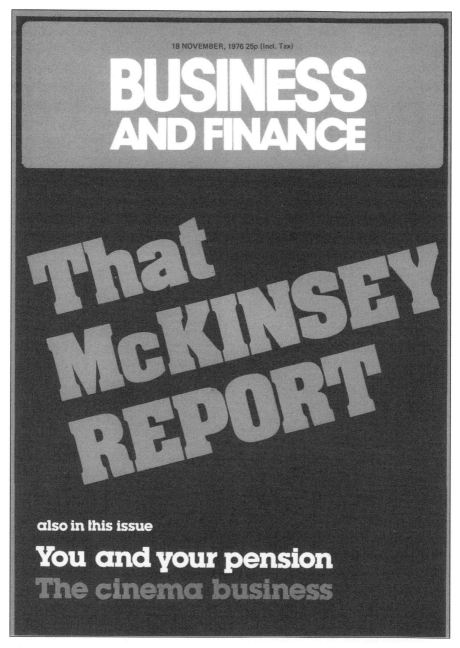

The 'McKinsey Report' published in Business and Finance *18 November 1976, Ireland*

By this time I had also served other major businesses in Ireland, including Guinness, Irish Distillers, Aer Lingus, Smurfits, and Waterford Glass. So I was visiting Dublin regularly, almost weekly, and had a widening circle of business contacts there.

The Republic of Ireland is a small country and has the benefit of a relatively small and close-knit business community. So perhaps I should not have been surprised when, at a business lunch I was attending in the Stafford Hotel in London, I was called to the telephone to take a call from Kevin McCourt, the CEO of Irish Distillers.

A second Irish National Bank strike had just got under way in recent days. Its object was to attempt to bring down the Government's national price and wage control policy, which it was using as a means to reduce inflationary pressures. The Union driving the strike action was the Irish Bank Officials Association (IBOA) under the leadership of its General Secretary, Job Stott. This union was unusual in that virtually all Bank employees up to and including general management were members. At that time it had a reputation for militancy and had not shrunk from strike action which effectively closed down the domestic banking system in the country. It would be an over-statement to compare the IBOA to the NUM in the UK at that time, but they did have the ability to inflict severe damage on the economy by inhibiting the continued circulation of money and the provision of normal banking services. At the time of the previous national bank strike several years earlier supermarkets and other retailers had stepped into the breach to enable cash and notes to circulate amongst the population.

So the Irish Government decided to take robust action. The Taoiseach appointed Maurice Cosgrave, a past Chairman of the Irish Labour Court and a past trade union leader, as its arbitrator, to seek to resolve the issues underlying strike action and to get the banks re-opened. Kevin McCourt, as spokesman for a small group of concerned businessmen, asked me if McKinsey would assist the arbitrator. The Taoiseach had blessed their approach to me. They wanted me to lead the McKinsey effort, given what they claimed to be my understanding of their economy etc. McCourt asked if I could go over to Dublin as soon as possible to meet Cosgrave and assemble a team.

I said that I must first consult my partners, given the obvious potential for publicity – good or bad – that might be of concern to the Firm. As I have indicated above, the banking system was fully unionised and the issues at stake were vital to the economy. Given the IBOA's reputation for militancy our involvement could well lead to unwelcome publicity. Having discussed with and secured the agreement of my fellow management group members in London, I told McCourt that we would be happy to help.

The next day I flew to Dublin. On arrival I was escorted off the plane ahead of the rest of the passengers, and taken swiftly through Customs to a waiting limousine where I was introduced to Maurice Cosgrave. 'We are so glad and relieved that you have come,' he said – several times. 'We thought you would not come.'

I was puzzled at the repetition of his concern and said as much. Then Cosgrave said, 'Have you not heard the awful news? – your Ambassador, Mr Biggs-Davidson's car was blown up by a landmine on its way into Dublin this morning and he was killed. So we assumed that you would cry off.'

I replied that, tragic and shocking as the news was, I had undertaken to help and was not going to be deterred by terrorist action.

I assembled a two-man team who between them had extensive banking experience to assist in our effort. Helmut Hagemann, a principal in the Düsseldorf office, and Peter Frank, an associate in London, were to support me. It was agreed that McKinsey's involvement should remain unpublished and that we should be presented as advisers only to the arbitrator.

The IBOA's relationship with the Irish banks was based on a national contract negotiated at national level. The contract under negotiation that year embodied a wage offer of a 2.5 per cent increase in line with the Government's guideline. It was this contract that the strike was designed to break. The real issue at stake was the Government's position, that any wage increase must be offset by an equal or greater increase in productivity and therefore some change in working practices. So our work had to focus on gaining a full understanding of the terms of the national contract and investigating areas of possible productivity improvement, as well as the nuances of each clause in the contract. To start this process it was agreed that we should meet the union's negotiating team and that at that meeting the Government's side would be led by Maurice Cosgrave flanked by two senior Irish civil servants on the one side and Helmut Hagemann and myself on the other, in an effort, perhaps futile, to withhold our identity. Maurice Cosgrave had agreed with us that there would be no reference to McKinsey at that meeting. Its purpose was to be purely exploratory, to listen to the IBOA executive state their case and the rationale on which they based their reasons for strike action.

So we duly entered the meeting room and sat on our side of a long table, opposite to the assembled union hierarchy of about six gentlemen, led by Job Stott, their General Secretary. The meeting got under way and Maurice Cosgrave asked Job Stott to explain the union's position and the reasons why they felt that they could not abide by the terms of the existing and proposed contract, and the Government's offer of a 2.5 per cent wage increase offset by improvements in productivity that had to be achievable. The two civil servants, Helmut Hagemann and I, remained silent as Job Stott proceeded to explain that the union felt it was an unfair position to be placed in and they felt unable to honour the provisions of the contract. As Job Stott continued, I noticed out of the corner of my eye that Helmut's jaw muscles were moving from time to time. Despite having some difficulty understanding the Irish accent, he was clearly finding it difficult to accept the rationale being offered by the union for riding roughshod over the terms of the contract and using them as the reason for strike action. A point arose where Helmut felt he had to make a comment, break our silence and thus risk loss of our anonymity. Quite suddenly he said in a clear but firm German accentuated English accent, 'We do not do it like that in Germany!' His words had a dramatic effect on the gentlemen across the table. There was a pause, jaws appeared to drop, and there was a realisation that very different experience was being brought to bear by the arbitrator in examining their refusal to accept the Government's anti-inflation wages policy.

There followed an intensive fourteen-day investigation of the union's assertions and the opportunities for improvement in productivity. This was followed by the speedy preparation of a report which was duly published by the arbitrator and led to extensive publicity. Large portions of the report were quoted verbatim by the press. These did not place the IBOA in a favourable light. The report and the surrounding commentary must have helped as the strike collapsed approximately two to three weeks after the publication of the report. The Government's wage deal was accepted by the IBOA, along with agreed action on areas of productivity improvement.

It was an unusual piece of work for McKinsey. It certainly put a spotlight on our work in the Republic and was a significant factor in getting the banking system back to work. There has not been another national bank strike in Ireland since.

One of the spin-offs from my work with grocery retail chains in the UK was a request from Tom Wilson to make a short presentation to the annual gathering of the Grocery Manufacturers of America Convention at the Greenbrier, near Roanoake, Virginia. At that time, the major UK retailers were achieving levels of net after-tax profit of between 4 per cent and 6 per cent compared to the 1 per cent to 1.5 per cent achieved by their counterparts in the USA. There were several reasons for this disparity. UK retailers had a more dominant position *vis-à-vis* their suppliers than was the case in the USA where there really were no chains with national coverage. Most major US manufacturers did have national distribution and strong brands well supported by advertising and promotion investment. This meant that the power or 'clout' in the relationship was more in favour of the US manufacturer than was the case in the UK. In addition, at that time systems used by the large UK retailers for stock control and distribution were in many ways more highly developed and gener- ated higher stock turns in the UK than in the USA. Furthermore the Robinson Patman legislation in the USA, enacted in the 1930s to contain the dominance of the Atlantic & Pacific Tea Company – better known as A & P – had prevented the development of excessive concentration of buying power by retail chains.

My presentation at the GMA followed on a session given by George Schultz, then Secretary of State in the Department of Labour in the US Government. It is on such occasions that one realises the level of interest in a presentation from a leading member of the US Government compared to one from a foreign consultant! As I took the podium I was acutely aware that my audience had diminished dramatically. Nevertheless I delivered my presentation which did seem to stir considerable interest as it clearly suggested that there were real opportunities for US chains to focus on improvement in several areas of their operation that could have a dramatic benefit on their bottom line and ROI. For example, to have increased stock turn by one turn could have delivered a near doubling of net after-tax profit.

In the early 70s I received a call from Don Carroll who asked if I would travel to South Africa to meet Anton Rupert at his home near

Stellenbosch in the Cape. He wanted to discuss ideas that he was developing for the formation of a company that would embrace all his various tobacco interests and operations throughout the world. He welcomed my colleague, John Beard, and me to his delightful Cape home, Fleur du Cap. He was aware of our work with the UK company, Carreras Rothman, and outlined his concept of drawing all his interests in tobacco together into one new multinational company which, if formed, would rival the two other leading companies in the field – Philip Morris and British American Tobacco (BAT). His companies included the Rothman companies in the UK, the Far East and Australia, Martin Brinkmann in Germany, and significant operations in the Benelux countries. These companies in turn had overseas interests of their own so it was a fairly complex structure and a real challenge to discover whether some form of combination of all these interests would generate a viable international competitor able to prosper up against very strong opposition.

Anton Rupert wanted us to test his hypotheses and if they proved favourable, to go as far as generating the actual corporate structure and identification of the funds needed to establish it on a viable basis. I remember querying as to why he would ask McKinsey to conduct all stages of this work rather than involve a merchant bank – particularly in the design of the corporate structure. His answer was interesting. He knew he could rely on our total confidentiality during this exercise and, therefore, did not wish to involve an investment bank until the moment was reached, if appropriate, actually to raise the funds for an agreed structure.

Anton Rupert was a fascinating individual; an Afrikaner, trained as a chemist, he had started up his own business in South Africa in tobacco products and wine production. From that base he had built an array of businesses around the world focused on tobacco production and marketing. Among those businesses was the Dunhill company, originally a supplier of smokers' perquisites, at that time quoted on the London Stock Exchange. Rupert was a man of enlightened views and I believe in those days in the late 1960s and early 1970s was a force for impending change in the apartheid regime in South Africa. He was also a most courteous host. Our discussions on that first visit ranged widely. It was my first visit to South Africa and Anton Rupert had arranged for some interesting and helpful sightseeing, to give John and me a greater feel for their environment.

I have to say that I found it very difficult to accept the outward signs of that regime and the complete segregation existing between white people, blacks and coloureds. I could see no justification, for example, for there being two separate viewing points at the Cape National Park – one for whites and one for blacks and coloureds. Such distinctions seemed unnatural and indeed unsustainable, as they subsequently proved to be. Nevertheless I have retained great affection for that part of the world enhanced when, years later, I had the unique pleasure along with my other Heinz colleagues of meeting Nelson Mandela when we welcomed him to Pittsburgh following his re-emergence as a world figure after his release from twenty-six years of captivity – but I run ahead of myself.

Our study took upwards of eighteen months to complete, at which point we felt a sustainable case had been made to set up a new company. It was to be called Rothmans International, probably based in Monte Carlo, along with a corporate structure that would be both tax efficient and operationally effective. During this work I had got to know John Chown, a well-known financial consultant based in London. A regular contributor to the *Financial Times* on complex tax issues, I had brought him on to our team as an adviser to assist in developing the most appropriate corporate structure. After considerable discussion and review a structure was agreed with Anton Rupert and his colleagues. At that point it had to be handed over to an investment bank to arrange for the provision of the necessary funds to launch the new company. Samuel Montague was to be the investment bank involved. We made a presentation to David Montagu and his colleagues and effectively handed over our proposals for implementation by Montague. Up to that point there had been no undue movement in the price of Dunhill shares on the London Stock Exchange. So it was of some concern to me that within two or three days of our presentation there was an apparent surge in activity in that stock on the Stock Exchange. I felt I should address my concern to David Montague privately, which I duly did. I received a somewhat ambivalent reply that I should not be surprised. Possibly, and with hindsight, we at McKinsey had been naive to expect that the total confidentiality that we had managed to preserve over eighteen months should have apparently been breached so soon after our presentation. However, afterwards it left with me a lingering concern as to the standards of probity and integrity practised in some parts of the City of London.

At this point in my career in McKinsey I was getting great satisfaction from the client base that I was developing, the stimulating intellectual content of the studies that I was doing and the interesting client managements and personalities I was fortunate to work with. The partnership environment suited me with its forthrightness in debate and the integrity of the Firm's professional approach to its clients. The underlying need of any organisation to be profitable to survive and prosper was not foremost in McKinsey. The focus was on the top management approach, on doing the best job possible for clients and taking on an obligation as a professional to advance the art of good management. This may sound over the top to many but it did represent the underlying philosophy of the Firm so well articulated and practised by Marvin Bower. I believe it gave McKinsey its distinctiveness and contributed much to its pre-eminent position among top management consultancies, which continues to this day.

But there have been temptations to emulate the fashions of the moment. In the 1970s Donaldson, Lufkin & Jenrette (DLJ) became the darlings of Wall Street with their apparent financial success and the obvious enrichment of their senior management. Significant debate took place among the Firm's partnership as to whether we should emulate DLJ's approach and essentially 'go Public', thereby enabling the then partners to reap very significant financial reward from such an exercise. It was decided that the partnership should gather and openly debate the issue to reach a decision. So at a Partners' Meeting in Madrid the matter was debated.

Marvin was in attendance although by that time he was no longer Managing Director of the Firm. He rose to speak and by his words brought the partnership back to its senses by demonstrating how the Firm would lose its professional integrity and destroy the trust by which the Firm's share ownership programme was handled enabling each generation of partners to prosper and pass on that prosperity to those coming up in the Firm as they gradually divested their shares among newly elected partners. His speech won the day, demonstrating, in my view rightly, that any such action would change the nature of the Firm irretrievably, fracture the partnership and pressure us to become just another commercially focused operation.

We may have lost one or two partners who were attracted to DLJ and similar organisations, but that decision enabled us to maintain our professional approach and continue to provide the means of broadening the partnership through broader share ownership and enhanced book value as the Firm continued to prosper and grow.

CHAPTER 9

A million mothers every day open a can of beans and say: 'Beanz Meanz Heinz'

A 1960s advertising jingle by Young and Rubicam

THE H.J. HEINZ COMPANY LIMITED, the British subsidiary of the Pittsburgh parent, contributed the lion's share of the Corporation's earnings in the 1960s and was without doubt one of the jewels in the Heinz crown. In 1963 Henry J. Heinz, the grandson of the founder, had handed over Chief Executive Officer responsibility to R. Burt Gookin, retaining the Chairman's role. During the early 1960s Burt had overseen the establishment of first class financial controls and planning systems across the Corporation. In that role he had been assisted by Don McVay, a McKinsey Consultant with whom I had worked on planning studies in the UK in the mid 60s. Don had joined Heinz in 1965 as Senior Vice-President Corporate Development at the Corporation's World Headquarters in Pittsburgh.

As was the case with so many of my McKinsey colleagues, we became good friends. He was a man of high integrity – always ready to speak his mind but also demonstrating great kindness and thoughtfulness with a great concern for the welfare of others. Carl Hoffman, a Director in the New York office, was at that time in charge of McKinsey's relationship with Heinz. Another Director, Everett Smith, had also worked closely with Jack Heinz.

In 1968 when I was a Principal, Don McVay asked me to carry out a study of the British company. Tony Beresford, then its Managing Director, acquiesced and the work was undertaken. As I have commented earlier, Heinz UK had experienced a period of significant growth in the early 1960s, going from strength to strength with increased market shares consolidating its position as one of the UK's most prestigious companies.

My team's findings were critical of certain aspects of new product development and signs of slowing sales growth. At Carl Hoffman's request I wrote a confidential memorandum to him noting various concerns. Shortly thereafter I was asked to meet Carl and Burt

Gookin in Pittsburgh to review the memorandum's contents. It was evident that some management changes at the British company were under consideration.

Later that year I had a call from someone I had not met before. His name was Tony O'Reilly, then working as Managing Director of the Irish Sugar Company in Dublin, Ireland. Tony said that he would be in London the following week and he would like to meet me for dinner while he was in London. We met in Bentley's restaurant in Beauchamp Place in central London. There, he told me that he was going to join Heinz UK early in 1969 as its Managing Director and that he had seen my memorandum and had discussed it with Carl Hoffman and Bert Gookin.

Terrible to report that up to that point I had never been an ardent observer of rugby football and of its star players at international level, so I was blissfully unaware that I was dining with Ireland's world-renowned winger, doyen of the British Lions, along with other rugby greats such as Cliff Morgan and J.P.R. Williams.

I found him excellent company. During our dinner discussion he asked me if I would give him some consulting help as he formulated his plans for change that he wanted to accomplish at Heinz UK.

So, shortly after Tony O'Reilly's appointment as Managing director of H.J. Heinz Company Limited, I assembled our team and we started work. Bob Lackey from the San Francisco office was our Engagement Manager and we assembled a strong study team which included John Banham, Sam Newington and Peter Foy.

Tony hit the ground running and soon was changing work habits, introducing a brisker pace into all areas of the business. He reported to Junius (Junie) Allan who as Senior Vice-President Europe had taken over from Fred Crabb a year or two earlier.

I believe our work was helpful to Tony and after six months at the end of the study Tony suggested that I leave McKinsey and join Heinz, with the prospect of taking over from him as it was already clear that he would be bound for World Headquarters in Pittsburgh at some point in the not too far distant future.

As with so many of those individuals who worked with Tony we had become good friends as well as working colleagues, aided perhaps by my familiarity with the business scene in Ireland. Una and I and our children had enjoyed his and Susan's hospitality at his home, Columbia, in Dalgeny near Dublin. So I was initially attracted by his suggestion. However, at that point in my McKinsey career I was still only a Principal or Junior Partner and the omens for my further advancement in the Firm seemed to be good. I also had my own base of clients and was able to generate additional studies and introduce new clients. All of this was delivering satisfactory and growing financial reward to me so I declined but did respond to his request to provide help when asked by him.

In 1971, to no-one's surprise, Tony and his family left their house in the UK for Heinz World Headquarters in Pittsburgh where he took up duties as Senior Vice-President in charge of Asia. John Connell took over Europe from Junie Allan, who retired, and returned to the UK using Heinz UK offices at Hayes Park as his base.

Tony by then had set up his own investment company in Dublin – Fitzwilliam – with his close colleagues Vincent Ferguson and Nicholas Leonard. They acquired Crowe Wilson, a medium size builders' merchants, to use as a quoted vehicle on the Dublin Stock Exchange to acquire a portfolio of companies.

In 1972 tragedy hit the Irish business community. A BEA flight from London en route to Brussels crashed, killing all on board. The majority of its passengers were senior Irish business executives bound for Brussels to participate in important negotiations regarding Ireland's entry into the Common Market. Among those passengers was a gentleman by the name of Con Smith who was about to become the Chief Executive Officer of S.C. Goulding, Ireland's leading manufacturer of agricultural fertilisers. Its Chairman was Sir Basil Goulding, a once met never to be forgotten character, well known in the Dublin social and business circuit for his impersonal but readable Annual Reports, known as the 'Chairman's Bone'. The company had been in difficulty for quite a long time. In fact Basil Goulding had asked me to provide some help two years prior to this tragedy. I had had an initial set of discussions with him and his co-directors and had told Basil that I did not think McKinsey could be helpful, given the state of the business and the management challenges that I foresaw, in achieving positive results from any effort by McKinsey.

In the tragic aftermath of that crash Basil Goulding contacted Tony O'Reilly, inviting him to return to Ireland from the US and fill the now vacant CEO position and get to grips with turning the business round.

Tony did more than meet Basil's request. Within a week he had agreed a reverse takeover of Goulding to form Fitzwilton, which by now embraced Crowe Wilson and its several subsidiaries. Thus Fitzwilton had become one of Ireland's biggest industrial companies virtually overnight. Tony asked me to help in the reorganisation which had to follow, working with Jim McCarthy whom Tony had appointed as CEO. Needless to say, my second meeting with Basil Goulding was on a very different basis from the first one!

In March 1972, Una and I were en route to Acapulco to attend a McKinsey Partners' Conference there. We had planned to stop over in Tobago and also Barbados for four days rest and recuperation. When we boarded our plane in Tobago bound for Barbados I was aware of my name being called on the public address system. Time was tight so I thought, if someone really wants me the call will come again when we reach Barbados. So we duly arrived for the first of many subsequent visits to Barbados and checked in to our hotel on the island's west coast. As we entered our room the phone rang. On the line was my secretary in London with the sad news that my father had died the day before.

We decided we must return immediately and caught the night flight back to London. We also decided that my father would not have wanted me to miss an important Partners' Conference. He was always a stickler for keeping going under adversity. So Una and I made all the necessary arrangements for his funeral and the family gathered for the sad occasion, as his death was the last link with his generation's family and he had been much loved by them all. My first job in the preparations was to drive down to see Fiona and Rory at their boarding schools to tell them of their grandfather's death. They were deeply moved and only then did I realise fully how much affection they had had for him over the years.

Una and I then boarded a direct flight to Acapulco to attend the Conference. Providentially the four days r & r had enabled us to make the turn round.

The last years of my father's life had been very hard for him. His health had faltered in the late 1960s and finally I had had to persuade him that the time had come for him to be provided with full-time care and medical attention. After a number of visits to possible nursing homes, which I found the most shattering experience as they ranged from the indescribable to the just about satisfactory, I secured a room for him in a small nursing home close to London. Satisfactory rather than outstanding, he was well cared for there and I was able to visit him regularly and keep an eye on his progress.

Like many people in a similar position I could not afford to pay nursing home fees in addition to my family's costs of house and education and we were not in a position to provide the care that he needed if he were to live with us, so I had to sell his home and clear its contents to raise funds for his care. I determined that this should not ever happen to me and Una in our later years, given that we had also had to sell up her parents' home to fund the care for them when it became needed in their later years.

In 1973, Tony O'Reilly was named President and Chief Operating Officer (COO) at Heinz and Burt Gookin continued in his position as Chief Executive Officer (CEO). In 1974 McKinsey was asked to review the Heinz World Headquarters (WHQ) planning system which had originally been developed by Don McVay and which, like all systems, needed review and a greater level of sophistication. This study included developing a computer based financial planning model to be used in the preparation of financial forecasts and financing needs which were to be presented at Heinz' next WHQ Management Conference at the Wigwam in Phoenix, Arizona, in May 1974. A key issue to be examined was whether Heinz would need to increase its equity base to fund planned growth over the next decade.

It turned out to be a landmark Conference. J. Connolly, a Senior Heinz Executive who was to become a close colleague in the years ahead, presented a paper indicating that there were major opportunities to reduce the level of inventories amongst the affiliates by focusing management attention on increasing stock turn. The cash thus released would provide the funds needed for investment in marketing and growth. This finding became a fundamental element in the Corporation's strategy over the next decade and really marked the beginning of the increased prosperity of the Corporation.

Early in 1979 Burt Gookin retired as CEO, retaining a seat on the Board of Directors. O'Reilly was appointed President and CEO, taking up his duties in July 1979. Don McVay was set to retire also in 1981.

During the year prior to 1979 Tony and I had kept in close touch as his Irish interests grew and Heinz fortunes improved. We were meeting on an infrequent but regular basis for update discussions.

Early in that same year Tony approached me and asked me whether I would consider joining the team he was assembling, to serve under him as CEO. I had developed a very high regard for him, both as a skilled manager and as a person of integrity. I was also very comfortable with his tough but collegial and non-political management style that he was intent on building into the way that the H.J. Heinz Company would be managed as a multinational corporation. His proposition to me was that I should become the Managing Director and CEO of the H.J. Heinz Company Limited, the British affiliate, for approximately two years, prior to joining the Board in Pittsburgh, and moving to the US on a permanent basis as Senior Vice-President in charge of Corporate Development.

Of all the CEOs that I had worked with during my eighteen years with McKinsey, Tony O'Reilly was the only individual for whom I would have seriously considered giving up my career with McKinsey and moving into a new role.

For me, and particularly for Una, it was a turning point in my career – for a number of reasons. Firstly there was the prospect for our family of emigration to the United States, certainly for the rest of my working life and probably beyond, along with the impact such a move might have on our children's education and personal development. Fiona was 20, Rory was 18 and Jamie was 11. The next issue I had to consider was the change from adviser to executive; in other words, to where the buck stops. I felt confident that I could make the shift successfully given the experience that I had gathered over the previous nearly two decades carrying out consulting engagements with top managements in a variety of businesses and having developed in-depth knowledge of the consumer packaged goods industry, from the point of view of both the manufacturer and the leading retailers. The aspect of Tony's proposition that really excited me was to become part of the leadership of a high quality consumer branded business which had a great deal of up-side if the new team could deliver on the opportunities that clearly existed.

I have always believed that timing and luck play a large part in success or failure in most things in life, particularly in business. In the late 1970s average Price Earnings ratios (PE) on Wall Street were hovering between eight times and ten times earnings. Therefore if it was possible to raise that PE by improving the performance of Heinz along with an upward movement generally in the valuation of earnings on Wall Street, this had to be a very attractive outlook. Burt Gookin had established the solid track record of the Heinz Company with Wall Street and had established a strong foundation for the company's success up to that point by delivering steady 8 to 10 per cent quarter by quarter increases in profits. He it was who established the decentralised organisation structure whereby each affiliate management was held accountable for the achievement of its profit goals previously reviewed and agreed with WHQ. This allowed significant delegation of authority and placed a real responsibility on the Managing Directors and their teams in each of the affiliates to achieve those goals. The reward system was structured accordingly, of which more later.

Perhaps the final factor that contributed to my decision to accept Tony O'Reilly's proposition was my increasing conviction that McKinsey & Company was not an older person's environment, despite my enjoyment and deep attachment to the Firm, its values and the quality of my colleagues and Partners.

So, Una and I decided to make the change. I offered my resignation to my Partners and in May 1979 I left McKinsey & Company after eighteen years of dramatic worldwide growth, during which period the Firm had become a byword in the English language. A new verb transitive had entered the lexicon – to be 'McKinseyed'!

Una and I were given two unforgettable send-offs by my London Partners. The first occasion was an elegant dinner at Hugh Parker's London home which was made even more memorable when, after dinner and speeches, Una and I were led into a darkened room set up as a disco. A group dressed in black, wearing dark glasses, were playing some very good trendy dance music. Una and I stepped out and as the lights came up I suddenly realised that the lead flute player in the group was our elder son, Rory. Roger and Meda Morrison had arranged to have 'Aardvark', the band that Rory had formed with some other chums, brought up from their boarding school in Surrey for the evening. Despite now being a successful international businessman in his own right, I still believe that Rory privately nurses an ambition to develop his musical talents, now being reflected in the similar talents of his three children.

Several days after Hugh Parker's dinner, my consumer interest group colleagues asked Una and me to a special private dinner at

Annabel's in London. It was equally memorable and I am sure that it was the only time that this august establishment has ever served delicately presented Heinz Baked Beans on toast!

I have many times since referred to my departure from McKinsey & Company as something approaching what it must be like to leave Holy Orders. The Firm was, and I believe still is, a unique organisation. Unique in the consistent quality of Firm members, from its reliance on thorough and complete analysis as a major part of its output and because of its philosophy of enabling individuals to develop their own areas of expertise and accompanying client base. Yes, it was always an 'up or out' policy but in my view that policy is essential in an organisation which relies on the skills, integrity and competence of its staff in a way that is different from a corporate environment.

It was about this time that Rory's musical talents and interest blossomed. He had taken lessons in flute and classical guitar. The latter is a wonderful sound but a very difficult instrument to master. A point was eventually reached where although a delight to listen to, Rory decided to set it aside and focus more of his attention on popular guitar playing, which he enjoys to this day.

The flute was another matter. He worked his way successfully through the Associated Board exams to reach Grade 8, and one of my greatest joys as his father was to attend a school concert to hear him play two movements from Mozart's Flute Concerto. Accompanied by an exceptionally talented school orchestra, it was quite outstanding. The quality of the sound and the feeling that went into his playing made the event very special. It was indeed one of the very special moments for me in realising that music would always be there for Rory in the years ahead – as it had always been for me.

As a result of my extensive consulting work with Heinz since the early 1960s I had the advantage of having a good knowledge of its management, particularly in Europe and the USA, and an understanding of its underlying strategy as well as its major opportunities and challenges.

The H.J. Heinz Company Limited (Heinz UK) was a very special company within the Heinz world. During the late 1950s and the 1960s it had been the bedrock of the Heinz corporation's profitability, generating well over 50 per cent of corporate earnings during the early 60s.

Its consumer franchise and brand recognition in the UK were unequalled, with leading market shares in over six major variety groups. It had built excellent relations with the trade and was still an essential part of any retailer's product assortment offered in his stores. Despite the gradual rise of private labels, Heinz products still justified their premium prices, giving consistent superior quality over what were really minor competitors in these categories.

In the year that I took over as Managing Director it was already evident that trading conditions were becoming tougher in the UK for all leading food manufacturers. The inexorable growth of the multiples was well under way. So the achievement of satisfactory profits and sales growth at that time was an increasing challenge.

I inherited a very strong management team in the British company. Roy King, who was in charge of marketing and sales, had a wealth of experience built over many years with the company and was highly respected within the industry. John Hinch, my Finance Director, was as solid as a rock, bringing US World Headquarters financial experience to bear from his period of secondment there: a steadying hand in all matters financial, who never let me down. Bob Norman, as Purchasing Director, carried major responsibilities for ensuring the provision of quality raw materials keenly priced. He carried a particular challenge as the world's biggest buyer of the Michigan navy bean – otherwise known as the prime ingredient for baked beans. As the UK population was by far the biggest per capita consumer of baked beans in tomato sauce, and as Heinz UK enjoyed over 50 per cent share of the UK market, he was in fact the world's biggest buyer of this pulse. So buying 'right' as to the timing of purchase, the quantity purchased and, vitally important, coinciding with a favourable US Dollar/Sterling exchange rate, had a major impact on the reliability of budgets as well as the final outcome on the bottom line. At that time Heinz UK was also the UK's largest maker of tin cans, so the availability of high quality tin plate from whatever source was also vitally important. This importance was amply demonstrated during the British Steel strike in 1979/80 when knowledge of the worldwide industry was essential in maintaining adequate supplies during the period of restriction from British sources. Little known seaports assumed critical importance in keeping supply lines open and staying one step ahead of miners' flying pickets intent on throttling our supplies.

At Kitt Green, opened by Her Majesty The Queen Mother in 1966, Heinz operated the biggest food manufacturing plant in Western Europe. This plant and Heinz UK's other factories at Harlesdon and Standish were all part of responsibilities carried by John Bodmer and George Corrin as Directors of manufacturing operations.

There are several companies in the UK that although owned outside the UK are, in the eye of the UK consumer, viewed as more British than the consumer himself or herself. The Hoover Company of US parentage, and Electrolux of Swedish ownership were examples of this presumed Britishness. Equally, or more so, was the perception of Heinz that had been operating in the UK since 1908. Chairman Jack Heinz, the founder's grandson, was also an acknowledged anglophile and well-known on the London scene, which lent credibility to the perception of the company as a multi-national British owned business.

So as Managing Director of Heinz UK I believe there was serious belief amongst even close friends that I was in charge of the Heinz Company worldwide! Needless to say I quickly disabused people but it was a measure of the Company's strong position with the UK consumer, generations of whom had been brought up on Heinz Baby Food, Heinz Baked Beans, Heinz Cream of Tomato Soup, Heinz Tomato Ketchup and Heinz Salad Cream.

Indeed it was brought home to me by samples of consumer letters that I insisted on seeing, whether they were to register satisfaction, or complaint or whatever. One memorable letter arrived on my desk from a lady in San Francisco, who was obviously British by the references in her letter.

> Dear Mr Heinz,
> I can do without Jimmy Young. I can do without Harold Wilson; but I cannot do without Heinz Cream of Tomato Soup. Where can I buy it in San Francisco?

In my view that is the essence of a brand franchise!

At the end of my first year as Managing Director we achieved our profit goals and bonus payments were made to qualifying Executives. At that time bonuses produced a very muted reaction as the amount remaining after the payment of extortionate rates of income tax acted more as a de-motivator than as an encouragement to those concerned.

It was also a time when industrial relations in the UK were being strangled by the aggressive tactics of various unions and the difficulties that were presented to management and supervisors in trying to 'run their businesses'. For example, nowadays decisions as to the appropriate speed at which a canning or bottling line should run relative to quality and possible improvements in materials handling is a decision that can comfortably be taken by management after study and co-operation with foremen and line operators. In 1979/80 even such straightforward changes required the intervention of shop stewards, lengthy negotiation and possible compromise of the appropriate outcome. Sensibly, with the restructuring of industrial relations which was achieved during the 1980s, such attitudes are a thing of the past and a much more productive relationship exists between management, workforce and unions – to the benefit particularly of the workers involved. How long this better state of affairs will last into the twenty-first century is, I believe, a matter of conjecture. It seems that each generation has to learn its own economic lessons – a necessity but nonetheless a pity.

Our budget for 1980/1981 set the Company on a course to double the prior year's profits. Various new products and improvements were coming forward supported by significant trade and consumer promotions. One of these was a canned label collection campaign which offered the opportunity for schools to be awarded items of sports kit, e.g. goal posts, tennis rackets, sporting kit, depending on the number of labels collected by the individual school. The top prize was to be the award of a mini-bus.

So the reader can imagine my dismay when this promotion was featured in a BBC *Consumer Watch* programme which, under the sound bite 'Heinz Meanz Cheatz', sought to demonstrate that schools would have to collect well over a million labels to qualify for the top prize. There was potential for serious damage to the Company's reputation and an alternative strategy had to be worked out quickly. All credit to Roy King who came forward with a proposal that we should 'gazzump' the BBC Programme by re-launching the promotion with a promise of eight mini-buses – each to be awarded to those schools that could come forward with a poem or essay describing the reasons why they believed they should be worthy of an award of a mini-bus. A panel of judges was formed comprising head teachers from up and down the country, charged with judging applicants. The result was that a potential disaster turned into a significant success at a very modest incremental cost, more than off-set by the restoration of integrity of the Company's offering.

By this time I had been required to make a presentation to the Annual WHQ Management Conference on the outlook for the British company and my assessment of its position. Tony O'Reilly introduced me to my worldwide colleagues with the following: 'I am delighted that Derek has joined us as it is much cheaper to employ him than to hire him as a McKinsey Consultant!'

In May 1981 John Connell advised me that I had been appointed to the Board of Directors at the last Board Meeting in Pittsburgh and so I made preparations to move to World Headquarters in Pittsburgh to take up duties in July 1981 as Senior Vice-President in charge of corporate development and as a member of the Executive Committee.

CHAPTER 10

Towards a Global Food Company

WHEN, UNDER BERT GOOKIN'S LEADERSHIP, Heinz adopted a world headquarters organisation structure, it required that the headquarters organisation should be unbundled from the Heinz USA division, the original Heinz branded business in the USA tracing its origins back to the operation set up by the founder in 1869 in Sharpsburg, Pennsylvania. The WHQ offices were still on the north side of the Allegheny River in Pittsburgh in Heinz USA's headquarters building, known as the Administration Building.

In 1981, coincident with Tony O'Reilly's appointment as Chief Executive Officer, a decision was taken to take space in the US Steel building in Grant Street in downtown Pittsburgh. So when I turned up in Pittsburgh in 1981 I took over McVay's office in the Administration Building on the North Side. The following year WHQ moved to the 60th floor of the US Steel building and I settled in to my office, adjacent to Tony O'Reilly's, which was to be my base for the next twelve years. At that time the US Steel building was the tallest in the business section of the city, being at least ten floors higher than any adjacent building. Consequently I enjoyed uninterrupted clear views down the Ohio River over Point State Park and Fort Duquesne where the Monongehela River merged with the Allegheny River to form the Ohio River, which then meandered on through Pennsylvania and the state of Ohio and finally emptied into Lake Erie.

In my role in charge of Corporate Development, I had three excellent staff managers who covered my main areas of responsibility. George Greer was in charge of Organisation Development, which covered the development and co-ordination of corporate policies relating to management compensation, personnel, development and the monitoring of the management incentive program across the corporation. That system embraced approximately 250 managers worldwide and was the foundation for the salary and bonus arrangements across the WHQ management group and within individual affiliate companies.

Senior Vice President, Corporate Development, H.J. Heinz Company World HQ,
Pittsburgh. In my office in the US Steel Building

Corporate Planning was at that point headed up by Eric Johnson
and shortly thereafter by Walter Schmid. They were responsible for
the development of annual business plans that led to the corporate
plan and the evolving strategy. They also led the process of business
planning across each affiliate by providing broad guidelines to be
followed and highlighting the major issues that various affiliates were
requested to examine as part of their own planning efforts and that
would also address areas of corporate interest or concern. Each year
a World Headquarters Management Conference was held attended by
the Executive Team and the Presidents of all affiliates. Corporate
Planning was also involved with any merger and acquisition projects,
some initiated by this unit or in support of initiatives from elsewhere
in the corporation. It also took the lead in or supported the
identification and evaluation of areas of possible new business both in
the US and abroad.

The third area of my responsibilities was Technical Services headed
then by Dr Lee Harrow. He carried responsibility for agronomy,
engineering services, liaison and contact with the US Food and Drug
Administration (FDA) on matters relating to food regulation and the
co-ordination of Research and Development within and among
individual affiliate companies.

These three individuals, George Greer, Walter Schmid and Lee Harrow, were supported by a team of six secretaries and personal assistants. From time to time we did supplement Corporate Planning with a high talent manager on secondment from an affiliate company who would benefit from the experience and exposure to headquarters activities. This meant that including me and my secretary Judie Compher, the WHQ Corporate Development Organisation numbered no more than a dozen persons. This structure reflected our philosophy of running a world headquarters group on as lean a basis as possible. There were no other staff personnel to call upon and it required individuals in those management positions to be 'hands on' and competent. The Finance and Legal groups operated on similar lines though with necessarily slightly larger numbers. This policy made for a very hardworking and committed group which, happily, was largely bereft of politics and gossip or competing staff which in other large businesses, I believe, are counter-productive to efficient direction and clear-cut communication.

When additional skills or experience were needed to examine areas of problem or opportunity we used task forces drawing on qualified persons from the affiliates to lead or support the effort. Infrequent but regular conferences of key personnel in particular functions from across affiliates also enabled us to share information and establish informal networks among key managers worldwide. It avoided having excess and costly staff 'standing by' at headquarters and importantly ensured that actual operating experience was the basis for problem solving or exploitation of profit improvement opportunities across the corporation.

In addition to the groups I have described above, WHQ included three other Senior Vice-Presidents (SVP) who were responsible for the operational activities and profitability of the affiliate companies. In a similar way, each had a secretary and beyond that communication was direct face-to-face with the affiliate Presidents/Managing Directors who reported to these SVPs. Unlike Caesar's Gaul, the Heinz world was divided into four parts at that time – the UK and Continental Europe, North America, Frozen Foods and Central America, and, finally, Japan and Heinz tuna operations based at Terminal Island in California.

The Executive Committee under Tony O'Reilly's chairmanship met monthly in Pittsburgh on the day before the full Board Meetings.

The same executive group also met twice yearly off site as a Management Committee for in-depth discussion of strategy and review of other major issues.

Annual business planning and the resulting budgets were a core part of Heinz operational control and strategic management system and played a key role in the setting and achievement of financial goals and targets. During the second quarter each affiliate prepared its three-year business plan focusing on the relatively small number of key issues that were crucial to its future profit growth and development. Annual budgets for the forthcoming year were set in the last quarter of the current year. During the third quarter Tony O'Reilly, the Chief Financial Officer, Legal Senior Counsel and I met face-to-face with each affiliate's management team to receive their rolling three-year business plan presentations. Two to three months later we met the managing directors/presidents of the major affiliates for a crucial mid-year review of progress against the current year's budget. The focus was on the progress being made towards achievement of the affiliates and therefore in the aggregate, the corporation's growth goals relating to sales revenue, marketing expenditure, operating income and net income, along with balance sheets and cash flows and importantly corporate earnings per share.

Each year this cycle of meetings was carried out largely outside Pittsburgh which therefore necessitated considerable travel, either to the affiliate's home location or to a third party location. Therefore there was considerable opportunity to get to know individual managers worldwide, to acquire in-depth understanding of the businesses, their area of responsibility, and their potential. Inevitably, as a result of the lean WHQ set-up there really was 'no hiding place' for problems, crises or inadequate performance. It also meant that if a problem did arise in a particular affiliate it would almost immediately appear 'on the corporate radar screen' and would thus be tackled with expedition.

I have expanded on the above because, drawing on my consulting experience observing the organisation structure and the modus operandi of many large businesses, I believe that the philosophy of lean organisation, fast communication between senior managers, uncluttered and uncomplicated by layers of excess staff particularly at WHQ, together with a high degree of trust, openness and collegiality, as encouraged by Tony O'Reilly, gave Heinz a considerable edge over some of its more cumbersome competitors – no names no pack drill! I am sure it was an important factor in the emergence during the 1980s of Heinz as a highly successful global food company.

In the early 1980s Information Technology (IT) was rearing its head as an increasingly powerful technology with enormous untapped potential to improve business efficiency, lower costs and raise productivity across all parts of the business system. Every Heinz affiliate had by then installed and been operating for many years a variety of systems ranging from payroll to sophisticated inventory control and production control systems. Certain affiliates were still designing their systems with the use of their own computer programmers. Others were evaluating and purchasing 'Off the Shelf' programmes from software houses that were demonstrating real competence in this area. In many cases it was already apparent that the 'build your own' approach was showing its weakness in needing additional development in-house with its increased complexity and reliance on continuity of programmer staff. Software houses were offering turnkey packages and providing their clients with application training and, importantly, further development/updating of their systems packages. This approach enabled clients such as Heinz to secure the benefit of their much wider application experience.

By the mid 1980s Heinz capital expenditure on IT was becoming a significant item, running into several millions of dollars annually across the corporation. Given the then relative independence of each affiliate as it focused on the achievement of its profit goals, this independence started to hinder the examination of opportunities to share systems and reduce cost as well as capitalise on the possible operating benefits. Aware that we were at risk of under capitalising on these investments, indeed at risk of duplication, I took two steps.

The first was to establish an inter affiliate IT Group reporting to me and comprising the IT heads of the major affiliates in North America. Its purpose was to establish the extent of their existing and planned IT applications, and to discover whether these applications could be shared from one affiliate to another thus saving 're-inventing the wheel' and excess expenditure. It would also start to formalise informal networks between some but not all affiliates by allowing IT heads to get to know each other better and develop respect for each head's IT competence and therefore generate professional respect – very important if sharing knowledge is to be accepted rather than mandated.

The second step was to hire, initially as an IT consultant, Phil Lichtenfels who had recently retired from Westinghouse (another large multinational corporation with its headquarters, like Heinz, based in Pittsburgh). He had been deeply involved in similar IT consolidation work there but well ahead of our then position.

Immediately we started to discover areas of significant savings (what in the trade are known as low hanging fruit!). Telecommunications were contracted by each affiliate. By negotiating a national contract with AT&T which laid down stringent service standards acceptable to each affiliate, several hundred thousand dollars were saved. Payroll systems were 'standardised' up to the required standard which accelerated their adoption for some affiliates and also improved employment files and base data. These examples were not rocket science and proved the principal that co-operation could bring a payoff to each affiliate by reducing its cost and raising efficiency.

I also instituted a technical IT evaluation process for all IT projects involving capital expenditure which was incorporated in the Corporation's financial analysis procedure for all capex approvals. The IT Group also provided technical input at this stage.

One guideline that I learned was always to be sceptical of claimed benefits for a new system. Never take on a system that has not been proven as workable elsewhere (and performed close to a budgeted cost and timetable), and as a rule insist on purchased packages and do not encourage in-house systems development – search out and use software houses with proven track records in the relevant field of application. The penalties for disregarding these guidelines can be severe – over budget expenditure, long delays in implementation and thus loss of benefits. Governments have fallen into this trap too often at their taxpayers' expense when they have not had the skills to manage and control IT contractors involved in multi-million IT projects.

In the latter half of the 1980s Phil and I discussed the possibility of outsourcing our North American computer operations. Prima facie it was attractive as a means of reducing increasing duplication of software applications and IT personnel among North American affiliates, thereby reducing capital expenditure on hardware and also maximising the use of our specialist IT staff. We drew up a very tight specification to cover our needs including the definition of very precise service criteria that any outsourcing provider would have to meet, together with cost penalties should agreed service levels not be met month by month. This 'package' was discussed with several potential providers who submitted bids. Genix, a Pittsburgh company able to offer complete backup disaster computer facilities, was finally hired. Each affiliate was a very hard task master in monitoring the service provided by Genix in meeting its requirements which put proper pressure on Genix. There were teething problems handled by a Heinz Genix joint working group set up for the purpose and over time the outsourcing was justified and met the goals we had set in first considering what has now become the norm for many corporations.

One of the valuable developments in the early 1980s that emanated from Japan, then worshipped as the apogee of management skill, was the concept of JIT or Just In Time. Developed initially in car production, its ideas spread quickly to other industries in other industrialised countries. Like all great notions the concept was simple; if all the inputs required to produce a finished product – raw materials, ingredients, parts and labour – were available at just the right time in the process of production from raw material to finished product, massive savings could be made in holding inventories at each stage, lead times could be shortened and return on investment enhanced. The other necessary ingredient was for the producer to be able to have confidence that each input was of consistent quality and to the required specification. Thus came into being the concept of Total Quality Management (TQM).

During the reconstruction of the Japanese industrial base after the devastation of World War Two, an American, Richard Demming, had developed the use of statistical measurement to improve production efficiency. He achieved remarkable results and during the late 1960s and into the 1970s his ideas were developed further, along with JIT, and were incorporated into TQM. TQM was marketed as the real way to raise efficiency, empower all employees and challenge the received wisdom in all areas of operation. By measuring these components the cost of quality could be established and programmes established to lower those costs. For example, if you discover that 50 per cent of your invoices issued to customers are inaccurate and give rise to credit claims and corrections as well as loss of customer goodwill, then to eliminate those errors and their causes will cut by half the cost of handling the invoice, improve cash flow via earlier settlement of correct invoices, and finally will improve customer relations.

At Heinz one of my SVP colleagues, Jay Connolly, pressed for the use of TQM across the Corporation believing fairly that significant efficiencies were achievable. Undoubtedly he was correct in principle. However to adopt TQM required the hiring of consultants to set up the infrastructure/organisation needed to train virtually all employees in the discipline. To learn the new language of TQM – paradigms, cost of quality etc. – courses were held in all affiliates, Facilitators were seconded and trained and the administration reporting requirements also established.

As time wore on several of my colleagues, myself included, became concerned at the burden of the TQM infrastructure and the difficulty of tracing the benefits to be sure that they more than offset the costs of operating the system. I had always had a simple philosophy that every new management idea must ultimately be able to demonstrate that its benefits flow down to the bottom line, either as incremental profit or as improved return on investment. Also we were at risk of TQM taking the eye off the main ball of running the business to achieve profit goals. Inevitably there had been scepticism among some senior executives; the requirement for each of us to undergo a TQM course and receive our 'Qualification' added to the slight feeling of mumbo-jumbo – too much focus on procedure and not enough on substance.

TQM did raise awareness among all employees and did deliver some benefit but it was rather like the old lady in her grocery store in a remote village in the west of Ireland after listening to the Government official explaining to her how the adoption of the new decimal currency would work when adopted in 1971, who replied, 'It's all very interesting but it will never catch on here!' TQM was a bit like that.

The food industry has always had an endearing feature from a business standpoint – people's stomachs have to be filled. In the USA in the latter part of the nineteenth century and in the early 1900s, food manufacturers had got away with poor and in some cases adulterated food product offerings. Henry J. Heinz led the way in the industry in securing the passage through the United States Congress of the Pure Food Act in 1908. This was an important landmark in the food industry's development as it represented the first serious attempt to require all processed foods to meet acceptable standards of hygiene, and the use of pure unadulterated ingredients in their production and packaging. For many years H.J. Heinz had packed his popular Heinz pickles and horseradish in clear glass jars so that all consumers could see that they were unadulterated and also to attract consumers to prefer Heinz products and their promise of purity and good flavour. While this may sound far-fetched now, at the turn of the twentieth century it was not unknown for unscrupulous food processors to add non-food ingredients, such as wood shavings, to add bulk.

To meet the continuing pressures for growth the search for new products and new markets has always been pressing as existing markets develop and mature. Since its early years in the American marketplace, Heinz expansion outside the USA had focused initially on Canada, the United Kingdom and Australia, supplemented by export from those countries to follow expatriates' taste for Heinz products, in particular baked beans, soups, tomato ketchup and other condiments.

So it was in fact not surprising that a study in the early 1980s revealed that nearly all of Heinz sales – then some three billion US dollars – were concentrated in countries representing just fifteen per cent of the world's population where growth was running at between one per cent and one and a half per cent per annum, whereas Heinz products had little or no presence in the other eighty-five per cent of the world's population in Africa, Asia and the Indian subcontinent where growth was running at over six per cent per annum. Unlike European based multinational food companies such as Anglo-Dutch Unilever and Swiss based Nestlé who over the years had established businesses reflecting prior empire trading links in Africa, India, Far East and Pacific, Heinz had virtually no presence in any of those areas.

To address this opportunity the strategy of 'plant the flag' was developed. Its intention was to assess the attractiveness of these undeveloped markets and then search for suitable candidates to acquire, enter into joint ventures with or expand the use of agencies as the most appropriate vehicle for entry, taking into account the level of risk and likely rate of return that could be achieved over a period. Inevitably the 'hurdle rates' of return for such investments were set much higher to reflect the greater risk where Heinz was largely unknown compared to, for example, the acquisition of a small business in a familiar market like the USA. We also set other criteria to minimise risk but which at the same time would not discourage us from considering entry into these countries and capitalising on their much higher rates of growth. We restricted the scale of funds that we would invest in any one situation so that in total we would never put more than one to two per cent of our asset base into these opportunities. As I have indicated elsewhere we also required a very high rate of return to recognise the risk, including exposure to potentially volatile local currencies.

As most of these countries were new to us, where the Heinz brand had virtually zero recognition and we lacked distribution, our policy was to use joint venture as the preferred vehicle and aim to secure a majority position which would give us a distribution system, local management and thus a base on which to build the existing business and introduce Heinz varieties.

A joint venture is a different animal to a wholly owned affiliate. In the latter there is a direct line of accountability to the owner. Transfer of technology and management skills and conformity to the owner's policies and systems of financial control are straightforward. In a joint venture relationship – even where majority prevails – operational efficiency and the directness of control have to be tempered by the culture and views of the partner. These matters are usually the stuff of negotiation prior to signing contracts, but, however all-encompassing at the time, the nuances of different cultures and mores of the host country and of the partner organisation do come into play and can present intriguing situations as the new venture starts to operate.

The first such foray was into Sub Saharan Africa. Tony O'Reilly charged Dick Patton, then in charge of Heinz USA and Canada, with the task of tackling Africa.

In 1981 at Lancaster House in London the country then known as Southern Rhodesia gained its independence, changing its name to Zimbabwe and a new government was established under President Robert Mugabe. As part of its new commercial credo, Mugabe had laid down that in the new order no foreign country would henceforward be allowed to achieve more than a forty-nine per cent ownership position in any Zimbabwean business. In 1980, Zimbabwe was probably the most advanced economy after South Africa in the region. Ten years under the Unilateral Declaration of Independence

(UDI) of the Smith regime, it had held its economy together with creative efforts by the farming and business community to overcome Western imposed economic sanctions. Probably its most important achievement was to have developed a world competitive farming industry whose key products of maize and tobacco both fed the population and helped feed neighbouring poorer countries via food exports and in addition generate foreign exchange as one of the world's major suppliers of quality tobacco leaf. Yields and standards of agronomy were world class.

Outside the then approximately 250,000 white population, the main staple of life among the black African population was maize used in the preparation of mealie meal, along with cooking oils and fats, and soap products for basic hygiene and cleanliness. Given Tony O'Reilly's reputation as a British Lions player in the 1955 Lions tour of South Africa and Southern Rhodesia, the combination of his contacts and Dick's efforts focused quickly on Olivine Industries – one of the largest food companies in the country with dominant market shares in cooking oils, margarine, soaps and candle manufacture. It also enjoyed a healthy export business to its neighbours in Zambia, Zaire, Angola and Mozambique. With good management and plant serviceable, although somewhat exhausted after the ten years of UDI sanctions, it offered us a base on which to build a business in Southern Africa and provide a vehicle to introduce over time appropriate Heinz varieties. In addition there was the possibility of working with leading local farmers to test the development and possible production of the Michigan pea bean, therefore providing a possible additional source of supply to Heinz UK.

At that time, the political and economic atmosphere was most encouraging – indeed exciting. Mugabe had stated his goal of drawing on all sections of the community – black, Asian and white – in developing the country and the mood, particularly among the 5,000 or so white farmers on whom the economy's viability and prosperity depended, was cautious but broadly optimistic. They liked what they heard and were prepared to work with the new regime. This was impressive as many of these individuals had been on the other side during the Civil War that preceded independence and were prepared to believe that Mugabe was a man they could work with.

Our negotiations went well. But inevitably we ran into the roadblock regarding our insistence on securing at least a fifty-one per cent majority if we were to succeed in purchasing Olivine. I made my first visit to Harare in 1982 as one of a small group of senior Heinz executives that went to get the feel of the country and the business community and assess the political climate. We were given a warm welcome and entertained by several other companies with whom Tony and Dick Patton had had preliminary discussions.

As I have said elsewhere, I am a strong believer in the importance of luck in the development of business strategy and its successful execution. At this time Don Wiley, Senior Vice-President and Heinz legal Counsel, was on a business trip through London. At the airport news stand a paperback volume caught his eye. It was a biography of Robert Mugabe – then, as now, much in the news although for vastly different reasons at that time. He purchased a copy and on reading it he discovered that as a boy Mugabe had been taught by a Jesuit Father. On mentioning this fact to Tony O'Reilly the latter realised that he too had been taught by the same Jesuit in Ireland. Together with our strong arguments for majority control I am sure this common link helped Tony O'Reilly to convince Mugabe of the benefits of Heinz participation and of the terms that we were offering. So the acquisition went forward, we achieved our goal of fifty-one per cent position with the government as our partner. As far as I know, to this day, Heinz is the only foreign investor to have achieved majority control in a Zimbabwean business, in part because of a lack of interest by potential foreign investors discouraged by the economic and political policies pursued by its government in the intervening years.

Over the years Olivine proved to be a good investment. Having secured the government's agreement to our ability to remit dividends, we had recovered more than our initial investment in the following decade. However, given the gradual deterioration of the economy and the collapse of the Zimbabwe dollar against the US dollar and most other currencies, it demonstrated the wisdom of associating with a successful business with a strong domestic market position. Ably managed it did provide the vehicle for setting up a plant in Chegutu to produce canned and bottled Heinz products including beans, pasta and tomato ketchup. It also demonstrated the political risks of operating in developing countries where the political environment is uncertain. Furthermore it justified our policy of restricting invest-ment in these situations to relatively low levels where we could tolerate risk or erosion of our investment and where a significant upside could more than justify the risk. In other words such investments had to have sufficient prospect of meeting demanding rates of return.

Coincident with our investment in Zimbabwe we had cast our eyes on the Pacific Rim – from Singapore to Japan. Only in Japan did we already have a Heinz presence. Heinz Japan had been a part of Heinz for over twenty years, starting life as a small joint venture. The business had grown from its base of Japanese style cooking sauces and soups and small quantities of imported tomato ketchup from Heinz USA: small quantities because of the then very high import duties and small quotas imposed by Japanese customs – perhaps to protect the dominant domestic based competitor, Kagome. We decided to enlarge our base so in the early 1980s a new factory was opened at Utsonomiya near Tokyo.

Tony O'Reilly, Joe Bogdanovich, Frank Bretthole, the Chief Financial Officer, and I attended the opening ceremony. Each of us was equipped with a colourful rosette on which was penned our name and position in Japanese script. We lined up with Mass Ogawa, Managing Director of Heinz Japan, to receive the four hundred or so guests in the car park at the entrance to the marquee that had been put up specially for the occasion. As each guest was welcomed he or she bowed graciously to each of us. Inevitably each one of us started to respond with a bow and so it went on until all guests had arrived. I began to feel like a bobbing Russian doll. We cut the tape and then when all were seated in the marquee the head of the Prefecture of Utsonomiya stepped up onto the podium to give his blessing to the new factory and its workforce. It was then Tony's turn to respond and welcome the guests. The head of the Prefecture was a very short man so a soapbox had been placed for him to stand on and be able to reach the microphone. Tony is well over six feet in height. He pushed the soapbox aside with his foot. The microphone still only came up to above his waist level and it refused to extend properly. So he lifted up the microphone and delivered his speech – a little reminiscent of 'Little and Large'.

The ceremonial barrel of sake was opened and supped to the cry of 'Banzai' from all the guests. It was the first time that I had heard at first hand (other than on film) the Banzai cry or shout – its intensity, sharpness and aggressive tone was memorable.

About that time Tony and I agreed that some resource should be focused on exploring and identifying opportunities to extend Heinz business in the Pacific Rim countries. The four Asian tigers (South Korea, Singapore, Taiwan and Hong Kong) and also Thailand and the Philippines were already emerging as high potential, high growth economies. Also, following President Nixon and Secretary of State Henry Kissinger's historic visit and meeting with Chou En Lai in 1979, the People's Republic of China (PRC) was showing signs of serious interest in foreign inward investment.

We decided to place a senior executive in the region who could bring in-depth knowledge of Heinz products and business style and philosophy to the search for suitable acquisition or joint venture opportunities in those markets. We agreed that I should approach Roy King, then still in position as Marketing Director at Heinz UK with over twenty years of Heinz experience. After discussion he accepted my offer and moved to Tokyo using Heinz Japan offices as his base.

It also seemed appropriate to try and arrange a briefing session for our executives with businessmen who were well steeped in that region. I remembered that an Emmanuel contemporary of mine, Bill Downey, was by then Finance Director of the Jardine Mattheson Group based in Hong Kong. He agreed to host such a meeting and the coincidence that he had played rugby at International level with Tony O'Reilly also helped. This session, along with similar briefings in Taiwan, was helpful.

It was quite normal for my office in Pittsburgh to receive enquiries from various parts of the world seeking to interest Heinz in various investment opportunities. Our normal practice in response to most of these was to forward a copy of our Annual Report and an acknowledging note so that if it became appropriate to follow up in due course, at least we had responded to that contact. In 1983, Ben Fisher in our Corporate Planning group received such an enquiry from a Mr Y.C. Wong, a Chinese trader based in Hong Kong, enquiring as to our interest in developing business in the People's Republic of China. Ben had sent the agreed acknowledgement and filed it away. Some time afterwards Roy King and I had agreed to make a series of exploratory visits to these countries. Before leaving Pittsburgh I stuffed our Y.C. Wong correspondence into my briefcase. On arrival in Hong Kong we made contact with Mr Wong and agreed to meet him in the cocktail bar of the Mandarin Hotel in Hong Kong. He turned out to be a very jovial gentleman, claiming to have entree to the powers-that-be in Guangzhou in the southern province of Guangdong. We agreed to meet him again to follow up on the area we had discussed – babyfood. Roy and I discussed our approach and it was agreed that Roy would meet Y.C. Wong, in future to be known as 'Y.C.', and indicate our serious potential interest in entering the virtually non-existent market for baby food in China. We believed that it was an area where Heinz' long-standing understanding of infant nutrition and the improvements in the removal of serious infant disabilities, such as rickets and poor bone structure, that Heinz knowledge and products had contributed to over the previous half century in North America and the UK, was experience that we could bring to a country where sadly the majority of mothers were unable to breast-feed their babies as a result of poor nutrition, or only able to feed their babies with *congee* – a sort of gruel composed of rice boiled in water where most of the limited nutrient was boiled away in the cooking process.

So I returned to Pittsburgh and Roy King made his first visit to China for initial discussion with Y.C. He and I had agreed that our strategy for those initial discussions would be to seek a majority shareholding in a joint venture with the goal of establishing a Heinz brand in Guangdong province and that we should seek to have protection from similar ventures for at least five years to enable us to establish the business position of the Heinz brand on the mainland and establish an infant nutrition programme in conjunction with local health authorities, hospitals and clinics.

Roy called me from Guangzhou after his meeting with Y.C. to report that the Chinese would probably agree to all our points. This was a more positive reaction than we had dared hope for so I thought we should build on that initiative and seek a similar position for all of mainland China – in other words not just confined to Guangdong province. So Roy went back in to his discussions and emerged a day later with the great news that it was quite possible for us to try to negotiate a position for all of China but we would have to go to Beijing to conduct the negotiation.

We now started serious preparation on our negotiating position and consulted Gerry Cohen, a leading US lawyer in the Hong Kong office of Paul, Weiss, Rifkind, Wharton & Garrison. Gerry had made a specialty of US/China relations and in particular the Chinese joint venture laws and regulations that were then the basis of any co-operation between foreign businesses and Chinese enterprises. He already had experience of assisting several US corporations in their efforts to enter the PRC.

In accordance with the PRC regulations we prepared an 'Agreed Memorandum' in which we laid out the points that we hoped to get agreed and be the basis for a joint venture. In summary these were as follows:

- Majority ownership – which we believed to be vital if we were to be free and able to bring in our infant nutrition expertise and our own experts. We wanted to secure a minimum sixty per cent position.
- A period of protection for the joint venture of at least five years – to allow the business to get established before other similar ventures were established in China.
- Adequate foreign exchange to be available for both importation of raw materials and dividend payments to the Heinz Company.

I arrived in Hong Kong on 16 February 1984 from Tokyo, where I had just delivered a speech and presentation to the Advertising and Marketing Association of Japan. I was joined in Hong Kong by Don Wiley, Roy King and John Mazur, a lawyer from the Heinz Law Department in Pittsburgh. It took us two days to discuss and refine the Agreed Memorandum with Gerry Cohen and his Chinese-speaking associate, Tim Stratford. On 19 February, Don, Roy, Tim, Y.C. and I left Hong Kong by train for Guangzhou – my and Don Wiley's first visit into mainland China. The journey of some 100 miles took over three hours. We crossed the border at Schenzen where PRC train personnel took over. With a TV at the end of each carriage, seating was comfortable, and attendants served green tea regularly – topping up mugs with boiling water from their kettles. As we rode along I was struck by the neatness of many of the small vegetable patches near the villages we passed. I thought it augured well for food cultivation later.

Y.C. had insisted that we take several bottles of brandy with us as gifts for our potential partners and the government officials we would meet in Beijing – apparently a much sought-after item of refreshment in China at that time.

Y.C. Wong, Roy King, RDF, Yang Lin in Beijing, 1983

My first impression on arrival at Guangzhou station was of a mass of de-training passengers and their luggage – most of which seemed to be in large plastic bags – trying to find those who had been waiting to meet them. We were driven away in Mercedes limousines, avoiding the literally thousands of bicycles that seemed to be the main mode of transport for most Chinese folk in the city. We arrived at the China Hotel, in 1984 a newly built twenty-storey building with its Friendship Store on the ground floor where only persons with foreign exchange were allowed in to purchase a variety of Chinese arts and crafts merchandise and cashmere garments.

The next day we were driven to the Agriculture Industry & Commerce Union compound to meet our potential Chinese partners. Y.C. and Tim Stratford acted as our interpreters as everything had to be translated both ways from English into Cantonese and vice-versa. Having two translators proved invaluable as we were able to keep completely abreast of discussions and the inevitable nuances. In a small room in the centre of a lagoon in the middle of the compound we met several Chinese gentlemen, among whom it became obvious that a Mr Dai Ye Ping and Yang Lin were the main spokesmen. Discussions were cordial and we appeared to be making very good progress and there seemed to be little opposition to the main points that were contained in our Agreed Memorandum. It was also becoming clear that our forthcoming visit to Beijing would be a very important element in securing national support for the project, as well as dealing with the potentially difficult position on achieving what the Chinese termed a foreign exchange balance. This phrase related to their concern that implicit in any deal should be the near certainty of generating sufficient foreign exchange, primarily via exports, to offset the foreign exchange requirement for the purchase of imported materials, packaging etc. From our standpoint in the early years such a balance was unlikely as any production was to be for the domestic market and exports were unlikely for several years. It was therefore important for us to secure comfort from the Chinese side that foreign exchange would be forthcoming in the early years of the joint venture to meet the cost of imported packaging and in time the payment of dividends.

In the middle of that week we flew on China Airlines from Guangzhou to Beijing. We stayed in the Jinguo Hotel that seemed to be the resting place of every other aspiring foreign businessman in Beijing. At that time we were also careful in any telephone conversations we held, either within or outside China, as there were persistent rumours that on occasion lines were tapped but I do not think that at any time my colleagues or I were so affected.

On arrival we went straight into discussions and met a number of senior Chinese executives, most important among whom were Du Ziduan, the President of the National Food Industry Association. That meeting was important as we were quite sure that we needed to get a written statement to give us sufficient comfort on the overall direction of the joint venture, and in particular the foreign exchange implications. So, on our second day in Beijing the Chinese had organised a sightseeing visit for us to the Great Wall at Kunming and a visit to the nearby tombs of the Chinese Emperors. With temperatures well below zero this visit was both fascinating and chilling. It was Y.C.'s first opportunity to experience snow, which required a stop to enable him to dismount from the coach and to enjoy the new experience. We also realised that this was perhaps the normal treatment during negotiations to give the Chinese side more time to consider their position.

On the last day of our visit we met President Du again and finally received the statement that we had been hoping for. So, with feelings of some self-satisfaction, we hosted a banquet in the Hall of the People in Tiananmen Square. This also was a new experience for several reasons. At that time all entertainment hosted by foreign visitors had to be paid for in Chinese yuan. Knowing that we were going to host a banquet I went to the Bank of China desk in the hotel each day to draw my daily allowance of yuan against American Express travellers cheques or US dollars. By the time of the banquet I had an inch thick wad of Chinese yuan stuffed into my breast pocket to be able to pay our final bill. The other feature of such occasions was the custom to invite all those individuals that you have met during such a visit to that banquet. At first glance this seemed to be a smart way by the Chinese to secure some free entertainment. Later it became evident that such occasions were all part of the familiarisation process and most of those individuals were at some point in the future going to help in the resolution of issues affecting the establishment and operation of the joint venture. I was to meet a number of our many guests on several future occasions at subsequent meetings in Beijing.

The final challenge of such banquets is the 'toasting process'. Throughout a meal of possibly ten to fourteen courses, it is good form for the host to welcome his guests and for the chief guest to thank the host and for the host then to visit every table for similar toasts as the meal progresses. Such toasts are often taken in a Chinese liqueur called *maotai*. It is derived from strawberries, and when taken in significant quantities can be quite lethal. The host has to be pretty robust to maintain his composure throughout the evening given the number of tables to be visited. Surprisingly all of this procedure is completed in a fairly short time. Guests would typically arrive at 5.30 p.m. and by 8.30 to 9.00 p.m. all would be done and guests would have departed. On this particular occasion we were dining in the Shandung Province Room in the Hall of the People where there is a reception/dining room for every one of China's provinces. I paid the bill and discovered as we drove back to our hotel that Yang Lin could in fact speak some English and indeed could render a passable version of 'Auld Lang Syne', supported by Roy King. It had been a successful visit. We were on the way to achieving a breakthrough for Heinz that would give the corporation a flying start in the world's biggest market and provide a base for a major food business in the long term.

Negotiations continued for several months. During this period a feasibility study had to be completed. Its purpose was to ascertain in detail all the aspects of the operation of the new company to be called Heinz UFE. This work included checking out all procurement requirements, ingredient availability and quality, packaging, skill requirements and manning levels for the new factory to be constructed. Ben Fisher, a member of my Corporate Planning Group in Pittsburgh, carried out much of the work, most of which was done in the PRC.

On 31 August 1984 in Guangzhou, I signed the joint venture contract on behalf of the Heinz Company and Heinz UFE came into being. I had been surprised, as had others, at the speed with which our negotiations had proceeded. I was well aware of other American companies struggling to secure contracts and taking many months if not years to get to the position that we had reached in six months. I believe the primary reason for this success was a straightforward one. China pays great attention to its children and its concern for their health and well-being. Of the eighteen to twenty million babies born each year, well over eighty-five per cent suffered from malnutrition. We offered not only a factory to produce suitable dry cereal as a supplement to breast feeding, but also a promise of bringing in our own nutritional experts to conduct joint studies with Chinese nutritionists aimed at improving infant health care and, in time, contributing to a better start in life for these infants. We did not seek a technology transfer fee and had been able to demonstrate to the Chinese Authorities the depth of our food manufacturing expertise in other product areas, which would ultimately be of benefit to China.

I made many trips to China in the ensuing nine years and found the pace of development of that country over that time quite fascinating. For example at our initial meetings, the Chinese side would arrive in plain Mao jackets. Women would wear no makeup and hair was straight and unpermed. A few years later Western ideas were prospering and Deng Zhao Peng was supportive. Western suits would be worn and makeup started to appear. Then there would be a cold spell with the West and you would sense it because Western style suits were replaced by Mao jackets etc. Those times are now past but they were indicative then of the faltering political uncertainties as China was opening up to the outside world. The economic

*'Well we got the Foundation Stone laid and the trees planted OK.' Tony O'Reilly
and RDF exchange comments after the ceremony, Guangzhou, China, 1983.
Una and Susan O'Reilly behind Tony's right shoulder*

*We open the new Heinz UFE baby cereal factory in Guangzhou 1984. Tony O'Reilly
and RDF ribbon cutting with much consumer help*

growth of that country continues to outpace nearly all Western economies. Without doubt in the latter part of this century, China will become one of if not 'the' dominant world power with its resources of people, its ability to take up new technology, and the sheer scale of the geography of the country. The attitude of many of their senior people was typified to me when I sat at another important banquet in the Great Hall in Beijing. I found myself sitting next to an Economics Minister and I made the comment that it seemed strange that I as a capitalist businessman was sitting next to and doing business with a Communist. Through the interpreter I got a very steely response that I have never forgotten, 'You must remember that thirty years of Communism in China is less than the wink of an eye in 5,000 years of history.'

The time came for the official opening of the new factory in Guangzhou. Equipped with the latest technology and specially designed product recipes it was at the time the newest and most up-to-date factory in the Heinz worldwide network. Jack Heinz, then Chairman, Tony O'Reilly, Don Wiley, Roy King and I represented the Heinz Company. Although Jack Heinz had stepped back from executive involvement in the business many years earlier, it was fascinating to me to see the impact made on our Chinese workers when they met Jack and, through their translator, suddenly realised that they had met Mr Heinz. It carried a special weight there and in many other areas of our operations and I believe was a valuable asset. There is no General Electric or General Motors able to have the same impact in those corporations.

We were very lucky as we developed our working relationships with our Chinese partners to be able to call on the services of several Heinz personnel of Chinese heritage and language skills who brought their expertise to bear. Dr David Yeung from Heinz Canada, who was our leading expert on infant nutrition, advised on the formulation of recipes for the new company's product line of baby cereals. These cereal products were fortified with iron and calcium to address the vitamin deficiencies in the existing infant diet. He also led the formation of the Heinz Institute of Nutritional Sciences that we established in co-operation with the University of Beijing. Under this programme, studies of infant early development were undertaken in areas such as bone structure to investigate the efficacy of the cereal products in improving these conditions. After several years into the programme it became evident that our baby cereal products were helping to improve infant health among newborn Chinese babies – perhaps the most rewarding aspect of the new business Heinz UFE. When I made my last visit to the company shortly before my retirement from Heinz in 1993, our Chinese partner was gracious enough to say in his speech that thanks to our efforts in getting the business established, millions of babies born in China could look forward to a better and healthier start in life.

In addition to the start up in China, an integral part of our Pacific Rim strategy was to assess the attractiveness of two of the fastest-growing economies in that area – South Korea and Thailand.

South Korea with a population of over forty million and, along with North Korea, known as the Hermit Kingdom because of its historic isolation from the rest of the world, had built a thriving economy since the end of the Korean War in 1956, in contrast to its ever more hermitic northern neighbour.

My first visit to the de-militarised zone (DMZ) at Pyongang left a chilling but sad impression with me. Looking over the no-man's land strip between the two countries and watching the North Korean border guard staring at us through binoculars, we were instructed to make no gestures whatsoever. The meeting room where the peace negotiations were conducted at the conclusion of the Korean War straddled the border so a walk round the table enabled one to visit both countries. The isolation between north and south was at that time complete. Since the Korean War in 1952 families had been separated totally by geography – no visits, no mail, no telephone communication. It was strange and terrible to meet businessmen who had had no contact with brothers, sisters, parents or grandparents for over thirty years. This personified the cruelty of the northern regime.

We focused our attention on a food company that would provide access to good retail distribution in the country. We secured agreement to form a 60/40 joint venture company – to be known as Seoul Heinz. It was agreed that a new factory would be built at Inchon – a fast-developing industrial site on the coast north of Seoul.

The factory was opened with due ceremony with a very well drilled Korean workforce. Dietmar Kluth, a Heinz vice president from Ore-Ida – Heinz frozen food affiliate based in Boise, Idaho – was appointed managing director and had moved to Seoul with his wife and children to take over what was to be a very tough assignment. At that time English speakers were rare in South Korea and Korean is a very difficult oriental language to penetrate, let alone learn.

We introduced tomato ketchup and other condiments to sell alongside the partner company's main lines of edible oils and fats. An unusual feature of selling in Korean grocery stores was the use of sales girls by the manufacturers. Their job in the grocery store was to check their company's allotted shelf space, keep the shelves stocked and assist shoppers in selection and purchasing of the company's products. We soon discovered that the loyalty of these sales girls was more than we had bargained for. If a shopper approached a shelf to pick up a bottle of Heinz tomato ketchup, the opposition sales girl would spot it, close in on the bewildered shopper and firmly guide her hand to replace the Heinz bottle to its position on the shelf and help the shopper to 'choose' the sales girl's own company product. This opposition required a large and expensive army of in-store sales girls, which added to the selling costs and squeezed margins in a very competitive market place.

Prior to the 1988 Olympic Games in Seoul, Heinz had been approached by the International Olympic Committee's (IOC) marketing agent to become a worldwide Top Sponsor. Each of our affiliates examined this proposal carefully to assess the potential benefit to them by way of increased brand awareness and sales to justify the additional promotional expenses that would have to come out of their own marketing budgets. Affiliate marketing heads attended a specially convened conference in Pittsburgh to report their findings as to the attractiveness of the sponsorship opportunity in their territories. The overall conclusion reached was not to go ahead with the IOC proposal.

The new Olympic stadium in Seoul where the opening ceremony was to take place was positioned on the banks of the Han River. Deitmar Kluth had also decided that even local support to the Korean Olympic Committee was too expensive. However, he remembered that we had used a large inflatable balloon in the shape of a Heinz tomato ketchup bottle at the factory opening ceremony at Inchon. Showing great initiative he had hired a small boat and had it moored in the river alongside the stadium. When the spectacular opening ceremony got under way up went the inflated Heinz ketchup bottle

– clearly visible above the rim of the stadium against a clear blue sky. The picture in *Newsweek* looked very good – an early effective and low-cost form of what today is better known as ambush marketing.

On my first visit to Seoul in 1984, I called on the US Ambassador at the US Embassy in the centre of the city. During our conversation I enquired about the security situation and the risks of any incursion by North Korea. After giving me a helpful rundown on the situation he added, 'Of course I should tell you that a North Korean missile is continuously targeted at where you and I are sitting!'

I wanted to get a better feel of the business climate for foreign investment in Malaysia so I contacted Ken Ohmae, a McKinsey co-director with whom I had worked in Japan. I knew that Ken had been appointed as an adviser to Dr Mahatir Mohammed, the Prime Minister of Malaysia. I asked him if he could arrange a meeting for me with the Prime Minister.

At short notice, Ken called me to say that the Prime Minister would see me in Kuala Lumpur in a week's time. As I was then in South Africa on a business visit I made speedy arrangements to fly to Singapore and then on to Kuala Lumpur. Imagine my surprise when after landing at Changi Airport in Singapore I was driven to Seletar Airport to take my plane onwards to Kuala Lumpur. It had a familiar look to it – thirty-one years earlier I had commanded a guard of honour of Gordon Highlanders on that airfield when Sir Malcolm MacDonald, then British Commissioner for South-East Asia, welcomed his French counterpart arriving for a visit to Singapore.

On arrival at Kuala Lumpur I was taken to Government House to meet the Prime Minister. For a moment it felt strange as the building had also been the seat of British Administration during the Emergency and served as General Gerald Templer's headquarters. I was ushered into the Prime Minister's office. A quiet man, dressed in *tongku* and Malayan robes, he impressed me as a quiet but determined individual. We had a courteous but rather remote conversation. Rightly proud of his country's development up to that point, he gave little or no encouragement in response to my explanation about our interest in Malaysia and our preferred ways of entering such a market. Following that meeting Roy King and I concluded that Malaysia was not to be a top priority in our Asia Pacific expansion efforts at that time.

Roy had found an interesting possible joint venture candidate in Thailand – Win Chance Foods. It was a small family enterprise with

Guard of Honour, 1 Gordons to welcome the French High Commissioner for South East Asia, Seletar Air Base, Singapore June 1952. British High Commissioner Malcolm MacDonald takes the salute

a factory at Bangplee, some miles north of Bangkok, and was capable of producing bottled goods including tomato ketchup. Ming Der Guan, the son of the founder, was to be our partner; a young and enthusiastic Thai Chinese with a good background in food technology. For different reasons we had decided to defer any serious investigation into Indonesia, the largest Muslim country in the region with a population of over 150 million. Initial meetings there had left us with the clear impression that service heads wielded significant power behind the scenes and the risks to Heinz were too great. As an American corporation we were subject to the Foreign Corrupt Trade Practices Act, which imposes serious penalties for any infringement of its provisions by a US company in a foreign territory. Corruption of any kind was to be avoided at all costs – even if it was to one's commercial disadvantage. Along with the interdict on trade with South Africa during the apartheid regime and similarly in South Vietnam, it did mean that companies from countries with no such prohibition on occasion were able to make the running to their early advantage.

Following the start-up in China, Korea and Thailand in the mid 1980s, I was concerned that the world's second largest populated country was still without entry options for Heinz. I had made several exploratory visits to India and had been introduced to a number of the country's leading trading groups among whom food operations always seemed to be an afterthought behind industrial products, machinery, and vehicle manufacture. These Indian companies were really vast conglomerates and did not offer worthwhile existing food operations that we might develop and use as a vehicle for the introduction of Heinz products.

Through Henry Kissinger's good offices, Tony O'Reilly and I had met Dr Tata of Tata – the biggest Indian group with leadership positions in airlines, commercial vehicles, manufacturing etc. These were all helpful introductions and deepened my understanding of the country, its politics and business environment. With a population of over 800 million and, unlike China, making no efforts to curtail a growing birth rate, it would one day catch up with China in that regard. About 150 million of that population enjoyed a standard of living close to that of Europe. The caste system still dominated society and I found it difficult to come to terms with the almost total disregard by those at the top for the abject poverty exemplified by the lower orders. It seemed wrong to me that you had literally to step over sleeping bodies on the sidewalk to get access to luxurious penthouses and mix amongst extraordinarily well-educated Indians. I couldn't resist asking one individual at such a cocktail party what he felt about the British presence following Indian independence in 1947. I was somewhat surprised by his reply. 'We owe you British a great debt for two reasons. First, if the British had not come to India there would be no India today and we would still be a conglomeration of competing and sometimes warring states. Secondly, without the British, we would have had no railways which provide the backbone of our communications across all of India!' I am not one of those who subscribe to the view that the British Empire delivered nothing other than exploitation of its subject countries. There is sufficient evidence, as I have witnessed on my travels, for the good that has been delivered despite fashionable claims to the contrary. The legacy of British concepts of law, civil administration, good education and of course the English language, still remain.

In the mid 1980s the Pepsi-Cola Company was trying hard to gain entry into the Indian market, ideally to be ahead of the Coca-Cola

Company, its bitter rival. One of the pre-conditions insisted upon by the Indian Authorities was a requirement to generate exports to compensate for the importation of its base syrups for manufacture of their range of drinks and to enable distribution to the local market in India. They had decided to set up a tomato processing operation in the Punjab with a view to exporting the resultant tomato solids. In our own efforts to find a suitable joint venture partner, Roy King and I had been made aware of the Pepsi operation. Indeed I believe they held out hopes that we might either co-invest with them to tap into our expertise in tomato technology (for example our agronomists had conducted hybrid seed trials in India for a number of years) or indeed purchase their operation as a base for our own future activities in tomato products in India. However we did not pursue this idea further.

Among the companies already participating in the condiments market in India was the food division of the Glaxo Company in India, a subsidiary of its multinational parent in Britain. A successful business already in condiments and infant nutrition products, it quickly became an attractive acquisition candidate for Heinz, coincident with Glaxo's concern to focus its efforts on its core pharmaceutical business in India. At a stroke it would deliver production facilities and good retail distribution and a product line that in time could be the base for the introduction of Heinz varieties. It also had the great advantage of good management operating within the disciplines and systems of its multinational parent in the UK. That acquisition was consummated after my retirement and has become a very worthy member of the Heinz family.

Concurrent with investigating possible entry into India, it was obvious that, after the fall of the Berlin Wall, Russia and Eastern Europe were going to open up to foreign investment to modernise their decrepit infrastructures and economies and, in time, to meet the inevitable increase in consumer demand for modern products and services.

Paul Corddry, then SVP Europe based in London, made an exploratory trip to Moscow early in 1990. He concluded that the time was ripening for a top level visit to explore a possible interest in Russia for the introduction of Heinz products – in particular baby food (possibly along lines similar to the Heinz UFE operation then up and running in China) and also canned foods.

In late October 1990, therefore, Tony O'Reilly, Paul, Joe Bogdanovich, J. Connolly and I arrived at Moscow's Scheremetyevo Airport to meet our Russian hosts and possible business partners. We were the first US corporate aircraft to fly into that airport – so there was a lot of interest and a reception had been laid on for us. In those days, the Russian authorities required that all navigation within Russia beyond Moscow should be handled by a Russian navigator whose job was to input all codes etc. into our plane's onboard computer. So Victor joined our three-man crew and stayed with us until we said farewell at Hong Kong airport following departure from Eastern Russia about a week later – some fourteen time zones east of Moscow, which underlines the vastness of the Russian federation and the variety of its cultures.

From Moscow we flew south to Stavropol in the Caucasus near the Black Sea to meet the local officials and get a feel for conditions, both agricultural and commercial, in the area where a possible joint venture might be located.

As we travelled in a motorcade with police cars flashing their lights to halt the traffic to let us through or to hold up traffic to keep crossroads clear, I was struck by the complete contrast of what I saw around me compared with what I had expected to see. The countryside was vast, bleak, and poorly cultivated. The villages we passed through looked as though they might have been locations for scenes from *Dr Zhivago* – broken down low wicker fences, mostly wood frame houses surrounded by estate farmland that looked ill-cared for. This impression was reflected in the sad state of their husbandry. We learned that they had 'lost' half of that year's tomato crop between field and retail outlet. Nearly a quarter of that crop had rotted in the ground for lack of labour to lift it, and a similar quantity had been 'lost' through the State co-operative system onward to the retail outlet. The quality of food available in shops was also poor. We visited several food stores. Their offerings were so poor: pock-marked fruit – apples and pears – most of which would not have been fit for sale in the US or Europe, scraggy meat, evil-looking sausages, and large jars of fruit juice. These shops, with their bald white-tiled walls and stone floors, looked more like public conveniences than places for the sale of foodstuff, with none of the variety and colour that we in the West have become so used to in our supermarkets. Some weeks after the Russian visit we invited several of the Russians with whom we had negotiated to come to the USA to visit some of our facilities and get a feel for our standards of manufacture as well as the choice offered to US consumers. While they were in Pittsburgh we took them to visit a typical US supermarket in Foxchapel, a suburb of Pittsburgh. The impact on our Russian friends was dramatic. They were overwhelmed by what they saw; the range and quality of products offered and the colourful and exciting presentation of the store itself was too much for them to take in. In fact several of them broke down and cried, so overcome were they by what they saw in comparison with what we had seen during our days in Russia.

During our time in Russia an extraordinarily competent lady interpreter who had an impressive grasp of English had accompanied us, and translated at each of our meetings. As is so often the case with interpreters, she worked through our lunches and dinners translating both ways. This meant that she had little or no opportunity to partake herself. I remember commenting on this to her after one of our store visits, worrying that she appeared to eat very little. Her reply spoke volumes: 'Please don't worry about me. We have all had so little to eat for so long that I cannot take food in quantity – my stomach will not allow it.'

Russians are very warm-hearted people and are equally warm hosts. After our second day in Stavropol we joined our hosts for dinner at their *dacha* – a log cabin tucked away in the countryside. I thought that my banqueting experiences in China had equipped me for any new challenging corporate encounter. I had not bargained for vodka. Seated at a long narrow table there were about twelve of us altogether, including our hosts. Thankfully, Paul had arranged for test quantities of tomatoes to be grown close by and available ahead of our visit so they were a welcome complement to the very solid food offered to us that evening. Almost before we were seated the Russian provincial governor rose to his feet to offer a welcome toast in vodka. Local custom required similar toasts from us – and so it went on throughout the evening, until the many bottles of vodka were exhausted and we prepared to leave for our hotel. Paul Corddry had warned us about the risks of a Russian bear-hug – indeed he had suffered a cracked rib from several on his previous visit. So we said goodnight and offered a handshake. Not good enough for our hosts. Each of us was clasped to a large manly chest. Two arms grasped you below the rib cage and tried with some success to squeeze the air out of you – at the same time attempting to lift you off the ground and plant a kiss on both cheeks. All of this is done to the accompaniment of convivial noises of mutual admiration. I do not think people realise what businessmen have to undergo in the quest for new business in new lands.

Our discussions were useful and set up a positive environment for future negotiations for a baby food operation in that part of Russia.

During our two days in Moscow prior to our visit to Stavropol we had met government officials in the Kremlin. It was a strange experience. As soon as you entered it was obvious that you were in a separate and different environment from the rest of Moscow. Run by the KGB, evidence of them was all around you. Dark green uniforms, highly polished black jackboots and expressionless faces watched over us as we moved from room to room along vast corridors. A special experience for me was to be shown round the Tsars' jewel room – showcases full of Fabergé eggs, richly encrusted vestments and the crowns and other items of imperial regalia. To me there was something inconsistent about a stolid Russian official showing us these relics of an imperial past with such evident pride so soon after the collapse of the communist regime that had slaughtered the last Tsar and his family during the Bolshevik revolution in 1917.

At that time there was one main hotel close by the Moskva River used by virtually all foreign businessmen visiting Moscow. Service was primitive, internal telephones worked sporadically and the inevitable large lady was in charge of each floor – keeping her wary eye on guest movements. Only one international phone line was available and it was located in the hotel lobby – so quite a high-powered queue waited, mostly patiently, to conduct essential business back home. For a change we decided to dine out at the hotel run by Finnair, the Finnish Airline. What a contrast. The restaurant décor was in the style of Maxim's, the well-known restaurant in Paris, and music was being provided by a young pianist.

Despite all their commercial problems, Russians hold the arts in high esteem and show great pride in their opera, ballet and music. For example, our hosts were most anxious that we should visit the home of Scriabin complete with the composer's revered relics – a visit that I have to say I enjoyed thoroughly.

As we ate our meal I was impressed by the pianist who was playing well-known classical pieces. So I thought I would try my luck and send him a request via our waiter. On a card I scribbled 'Fantaisie-Impromptu by Chopin' – one of my own favourites. A few minutes later I got my wish – played quite superbly. Indeed that moment characterised the great paradox of Russia, and perhaps its greatest challenge as it sheds drab bureaucracy for the competitive world of the free market where artistic talent has got to be matched by entrepreneurial flair and commercial acumen.

On day four of our visit the time had come for us to depart Stavropol. We had viewed possible sites for a joint project and had had full discussions, although clearly a complex issue was going to be any project's ability to generate foreign exchange given the inconvertibility of the Russian ruble, although interestingly at that time the only currency with which it did have convertibility was the Indian rupee. On the eve of our departure we dined with our hosts at Kislovodsk Castle. Here, each of us was made an honorary Cossack and presented with a cloak, dagger, and drinking horn – to celebrate our new status. To qualify for our honorary status we had to imbibe from our drinking horns which were full of vodka. With this challenge met and thinking that the calm of our aeroplane awaited us, imagine our consternation when we arrived at the airport to find that there was another farewell feast waiting – organised by the airport manager. Finally, back in our aeroplane, we said goodbye to our Russian hosts and took off eastwards towards Hong Kong. En route we made two refuelling stops at Russian military airbases. Here we saw the evidence of Russia's military build-up and began to realise the terrible cost paid by the average Russian citizen for their country's supposed superpower status. To me it was the equivalent of witnessing a great confidence trick played on the Western powers – sophisticated modern weaponry developed at a terrible and finally unaffordable cost to a population virtually on the breadline.

However, therein lay the enormous opportunity to help provide the elements of a better life for Russian citizens – one that we at Heinz in due course responded to, along with other US and Western corporations.

On arrival at Kai Tak Airport in Hong Kong we said goodbye to Victor, our Russian navigator. He had been a very congenial additional crew member who then had to make his own way back to Moscow, his Russian masters having overlooked making any return travel arrangements for him. In the afternoon after our arrival we took presentations by the managements of our Korean, Chinese and Japanese affiliates, putting forward their business plans for the next cycle; and then on the following day Heinz Australia presented its three-year plan. Later that day I left the main party and took a train to Guangzhou for local meetings there, before departing later that evening to Beijing. From Beijing I travelled to Tokyo to attend the Japanese Marketing Association's Conference, where I made a presentation describing Heinz' approach to marketing and business development around the world. I arrived back in Pittsburgh towards the end of that week, having been away from home for three weeks – a very typical travel pattern.

In 1990 the London *Financial Times* carried a report that an Australian company – Goodman, Fielder, Wattie – had decided to divest its New Zealand food operations, known as Watties, as a result of a strategic decision to increase its investment in the biscuit market in Australia. Over many years we had eyed Watties with a great deal of interest. In many ways it mirrored the product ranges offered by the Heinz Company in Australia. It had dominant positions in sectors similar to those where Heinz was strong such as babyfood and canned and bottled goods. In addition Watties held strong positions in frozen vegetables, ice-cream, and frozen and refrigerated chicken. I think that Tony O'Reilly and I in different parts of the world had seen the same *FT* report and we contacted each other and agreed that we would seek to acquire the Wattie company from Goodman, Fielder, Wattie provided an acceptable deal could be structured. I found this experience very interesting. My first visit to New Zealand had taken place in the mid 1970s under the auspices of McKinsey & Company to consult with the Freezing Companies Association in New Zealand who were experiencing severe industrial relations problems. It had great natural advantages of a clean environment by virtue of its distance from both Australia and the rest of the world. This was especially relevant as it enjoyed a strong trade in frozen vegetables with Japan. Like Ireland, cattle grazed on grass throughout the year and by 1990 it had transformed its economic environment by essentially jettisoning the welfare state by the removal of all agricultural subsidies and a transformed union labour environment from the one I experienced in the 70s when it seemed to be the final resting place for Scottish and Irish shop stewards.

For Heinz one of the most difficult industrial relations environments in all the corporation was located at Heinz Australia. Working hours were heavily restricted to 35 hours a week or less, shift patterns were restricted and walkouts and/or unofficial strikes were not unusual. As part of our analysis leading up to the acquisition of Watties, because of the similarity of production processes and equipment in areas such as canned meals and baked beans, we were able to conduct very accurate benchmark studies. These revealed that New Zealand wages were of the order of 15 to 20 per cent below the Australian equivalent per hour. Shift work was undertaken by mutual agreement by workers and management and, most important-ly, the employment costs or on-costs of an employee in New Zealand were between 25 and 30 per cent of wage cost, whereas in Australia, similar costs were of the order of 50 to 60 per cent. Based on these findings we were able to approach the Australian government of the day to seek their co-operation to work with us to bring New Zealand labour practices to our Australian affiliate. It was clear to us that if we could not achieve similar improvements, there would be little point in further investment in Heinz Australia and we would therefore have to consider focusing future investment on Watties. As Watties' Australian company had, at that time, seriously eroded Heinz' market position in Australia in ready meals and baked beans, this was not an idle comment. Within a few months Heinz labour relations im-proved. The work week increased to 40 hours and shift work was re-introduced. With a great deal of perseverance from Walter Schmid our negotiations with Goodman Fielder came to a successful conclusion and Heinz acquired Watties in 1992.

So at the time of my retirement from Heinz in 1993 we had largely succeeded in laying the foundations for Heinz' future expansion in Asia Pacific, China, the South Pacific, and the Indian sub-continent. By the end of fiscal 1993, Heinz worldwide sales had risen to over seven billion dollars and its market capitalisation had risen to over eleven billion dollars.

In 1989 the then largest transaction took place on Wall Street when Kolburg, Kravis, Roberts (KKR) bought RJR Nabisco in the USA. It had achieved considerable media attention not only because of its size at over $31 billion, but because of the controversy surrounding the nature of the transaction – one of the first leveraged buyouts relying heavily on high cost junk bonds for its financing. *Barbarians at the Gate* became a best seller; the first act for most of its readers, including me, was to look at the index to check that one's name was not listed there! KKR hired Lou Gerstner from American Express to become the new Chief Executive. Before joining American Express, Lou had been a Director of McKinsey at the same time as me. Lou and KKR approached Karl von der Hyden, then the Chief Financial Officer of Heinz, to join RJR as its Chief Financial Officer reporting to Lou. Karl accepted and left Heinz. Tony approached me to ask me to take over the responsibilities of Chief Financial Officer on Karl's departure. I held this position until 1992 when we appointed David R. Williams as my successor in that role. However, over that period from 1989 to 1992, I continued to discharge my responsibilities for corporate development but handed over direction of our Pacific Rim development responsibilities to David Sculley. I resumed those responsibilities from Sculley in 1992.

For some years I had had in my mind that I would seek retirement at the age of 60. I had had two outstanding careers: the first with McKinsey, the world's leading top management consultancy participating in its growth and expansion in the 1960s and 1970s; and the second with the Heinz Company, one of the world's leading food multinational companies as a member of Tony O'Reilly's senior executive team at a time when the company was generating over 21 per cent annual compound rate of total return to its shareholders – at the time a performance envied by most other US owned food businesses. It had been intensely stimulating and rewarding and I had enjoyed my close working relationship with Tony for over twenty years. But I had also realised that, with Don Wiley's retirement in 1989, I had suddenly become the oldest Executive Director on the Board and realised that there were other interests that I wanted to develop while still young enough to do so.

However in my discussions with Tony, he asked me to stay on to the age of 61 – so in mid 1993 my career with the Heinz Company came to a close. This had been a period of enormous enjoyment, working with a first-class Chairman and Chief Executive Officer in Tony O'Reilly and being part of a professional team that had seen the Heinz Company become the most profitable US owned pure food company and emerge as a worldwide global player in the food industry.

CHAPTER 11

There is a Life in Pittsburgh

W HEN UNA AND I AND OUR FAMILY left the UK in July 1981 for
the USA, we had already found a modern newly built house
set in five acres of grassland in Sewickley Heights, an attractive rural
community some seventeen miles north-east of Pittsburgh city. We
decided to install a swimming pool and tennis court to improve our
enjoyment and take advantage of the sunshine and warmth of
summers in Pennsylvania. The house suited us well, given my
extensive travels, and for Una it was an easily run home equipped
with all modern aids including a central vacuum system, and internal
air filtration, and with heating and air-conditioning control at the
flick of a switch. It was totally electric which also simplified operation
– except of course for the occasional power outages, which were
more frequent than we had expected.

Fiona was finishing her degree course at Bristol University. Rory
was already into his first year at Leeds University, and Jamie was
about to enter Cranleigh School as the third Finlay to pass through
that establishment. As with his sister and older brother he was to leave
his mark there in choral music, as well as a discus record that still
stands to this day.

The reader will not be surprised to learn that I have a very high
regard for how well-run US businesses operate and the style of
management that combines the drive and commitment that lies
behind much of that country's success. A concomitant of that success
at both the corporate and the personal level is the expectation by local
communities that they too will benefit from such success.

The Heinz Company was among the leaders in discharging such
responsibilities within Pittsburgh and the State of Pennsylvania and
elsewhere. As early as the late 1800s Henry J. Heinz, the founder,
had already provided a range of benefits to his employees that were
well ahead of the then standards of the day. The Heinz family, latterly
in the shape of HJ's grandson Jack Heinz, had given great financial
help and personal commitment to major civic projects in the City.
The corporation had also contributed to these and similar efforts

through the H.J. Heinz Company Foundation on which Tony, Don Wiley and I sat as Trustees. Heinz Hall was perhaps the most well-known of the family's contribution to City life. They had financed the complete reconstruction and refurbishing of an old downtown movie house, transforming it into a world-class concert hall. It was home to the internationally acclaimed Pittsburgh Symphony Orchestra (PSO), which was also well supported by the family and the corporation. In the early 1990s the Benedum Center, also supported by the Heinz Family Foundations, was renovated and opened to provide added opportunities to enjoy opera and ballet, as well as theatre in the City. On a personal level the contributions of me and many others came in the form of financial donations and membership of various organisations where one's business experience could complement the professionals charged with running such organisations.

I spent three enjoyable years as a Board member of the Pittsburgh Symphony Society when Lauren Maazel was its Director and Conductor. He had taken over this position from André Previn in the early 1980s when Previn departed abruptly to take over the Los Angeles Symphony.

As a regular attender at PSO concerts in Heinz Hall, I had always been puzzled as to why, despite rapturous applause at many of their performances, they never responded to their audience's enthusiasm by playing an encore. I got my answer to this conundrum in Hong Kong. The PSO had arrived there in 1990 as part of an East Asia tour, which was also to include a first performance in the Workers Stadium in Beijing of Beethoven's ' Ode to Joy' sung in Chinese by a chorus of several hundred conducted by Maazel.

The orchestra was scheduled to give two concerts in Hong Kong. I had hosted a small party for the performance and a reception and dinner afterwards at the Mandarin Hotel nearby for Lauren Maazel and the Pittsburgh party that was travelling with the orchestra. As expected the orchestra performed superbly under Maazel's baton, to rapturous applause from the audience who gave them a standing ovation. To my surprise and delight they then proceeded to play Beethoven's overture 'Prometheus' as an encore. They even followed it with a second encore and both Lauren Maazel and the orchestra seemed to be thoroughly enjoying themselves as much as their audience.

Maestro Maazel joined us at the reception after the concert. In my words of welcome and thanks to the PSO, I asked Maazel why I had to travel halfway round the world to elicit an encore from the PSO – something that none of us had succeeded in getting them to give us in Pittsburgh. The maestro rose to reply, and with a twinkle in his eye said, 'I will tell you why we do not give encores in Heinz Hall in Pittsburgh. When we perform in the USA we are bound by the prevailing agreement with the US Musicians' Union. This allows us to play for a finite time at each performance. Going beyond that time requires the payment of an overtime premium. No such rule applies when we are abroad!' Needless to say their 'Ode to Joy' performance in Beijing was also rewarded by an encore.

I also enjoyed serving on the Board of the Pittsburgh Public Theatre, which gave support to more controversial theatrical presentations in the City. Other extramural activities also included acting as Chairman of the Board of Visitors at the Department of International Studies at the University of Pittsburgh, working with its then Director, Dr Burkhart Holzner. I have always had a concern that academia, while discharging its role in research and the expansion of knowledge, often becomes too remote from the real world of commerce – the world into which so many of its students will ultimately enter. Establishing a good balance between interest and relevance is an important challenge for tutor as well as student. The Board of Visitors met annually for two days, during which we heard presentations from the Heads of each Faculty in the Department. Each Head described the range and subject matter of the syllabus he or she was teaching. The Board comprised six other senior business executives who, like myself, were drawn from other multinational corporations also based in Pittsburgh. These meetings generated a valuable exchange of views, helpful both to the academics and to the businessmen present. I believe it did help sharpen the focus of the Department's curriculum and teaching, and therefore make it more relevant and useful to its students.

I spent ten years as a Trustee of the Mercy Hospital in Pittsburgh, which included membership of its Finance Committee. Having experienced the National Health Service in the UK for over forty years with its underlying concept of medical care, free to all at the point of need, I was also aware of the ongoing criticism of the United States health care system by sections of the UK establishment. My service as Trustee of a US hospital was a fascinating opportunity to see how the US approach worked and to get a feel for its strengths as well as its weaknesses compared to the UK. Much is made by its UK critics of the claim that over thirty million American citizens have no access to medical insurance cover and therefore, beyond the limited provisions of Medicare and Medicaid, these individuals are at the mercy of unscrupulous charges for major medical care that are well beyond their means or ability to pay. They are therefore denied access to quality health care when it is most needed.

As I learned, virtually all US employers provide health insurance for their employees. Such cover provides varying degrees of care and is often supplemented by the individual if he or she wants to provide additional cover for ailments excluded from an employer's plan. Indeed it is an item taken very seriously by Trade Unions in their wage bargaining negotiations. One result of this situation was that a hospital such as Mercy, operated by the Sisters of Mercy, quickly focused on the level of charges made by doctors and other professionals for each type of treatment or surgery that was offered within the Mercy Hospital system to ensure that such charges were competitive and of quality.

Mercy's mission was to provide care for all who came to its door, including those without insurance. It sought to achieve that goal in several ways. The three major items in its budget were drugs, nursing costs, and doctors' and surgeons' fees. The number and type of each surgical procedure was analysed, costed and used as the basis for its annual budget process. However, the resulting charges for individual treatments also included an additional margin that, over time, provided a 'fund' that was available to pay for treatment needed by those patients seeking help who had no insurance cover or inadequate means to pay for treatment.

Major capital requirements were met by fund-raising campaigns that sought contributions from individual hospital trustees, local individuals and company foundations, along with the many foundations operated by the founding families in Pittsburgh. This meant that there was a local character to both the funding and the provision of care in the community. Mercy was one of four major hospitals in Pittsburgh serving the greater Pittsburgh area, supported by several smaller hospitals in some of the smaller surrounding communities. Necessarily, therefore, it was in competition with those other institutions and thus there was concern always to offer competitive high standards of care, supported by top-class medical professionals working with access to the latest technology and utilising modern updated capital plant.

There is no equivalent in the United States of the British general practitioner. So for Una and me and our family it was necessary early on to ascertain who was the best physician to turn to for treatment of a particular ailment. Although different to the UK system this approach meant that you could go direct to the specialist concerned without delay – a distinct advantage – although in our case it took a little while to 'suss out' these points of contact.

The NHS concept in the UK is a precious asset but the cumbersome nature of its Soviet style organisation controlled central-ly by politicians, not medical professionals, is an expensive anomaly that costs the nation dear and inevitably harbours bureaucratic inefficiency. Until the UK is able to evaluate alternative funding mechanisms and methods of delivery, free of ideological baggage and political interference, patients – the whole point of the exercise – will continue to be denied access to really world class medical care on a par with its European and US peers. The US approach is not perfect and its biggest weakness was and still is the burgeoning cost of health care insurance to be met by employers and others. Efforts to control those costs have meant that a 'cafeteria' approach has been adopted by many insurance programs that allows the individual to pay extra for elements of care not included in an employer's plan.

In November 1990 Una and I and our family were to experience the quality of US health care in a way that we could not have anticipated. Una and I were away on a five-week business trip in Asia and had reached Hong Kong. Una phoned Jamie, then in his second year at the University of Pittsburgh, to catch up on news. He said he had been to the University Medical Centre bothered about a swelling in his neck – wondering whether or not it might be mumps. Una suggested that he go straight to Mercy Hospital to have it checked. The hospital wanted to keep him in under observation but as he was due to meet us at the airport he was concerned that if he did not show up we would immediately become worried. The following day he was admitted for observation. When visiting Jamie in his hospital room we were joined by his doctor and a specialist who turned out to be an oncologist. They told the three of us that Jamie had suspected cancer and that tests were to be carried out immediately to establish the exact type of cancer. They suspected Hodgkin's disease, which is among the most treatable of cancers of the lymph system if diagnosed early enough and treated immediately. After tests of his blood, and biopsies of his bone marrow, liver and kidney, they confirmed that Jamie had Stage One Hodgkin's, which had a 90 per cent chance of full recovery, being the most treatable type and having been diagnosed early. They wanted treatment to start immediately and offered either chemotherapy or radiation of the lymph system. Jamie opted for intense radiation rather than the longer duration chemotherapy treatment. So for the next two months he undertook daily high doses of radiation. The effects on him were tough; the biggest sunburn I have ever seen developed on his shoulders and upper back, he lost his appetite and taste, and experienced severe difficulty in swallowing. Radiation had to be applied to the whole lymph system – unlike the then prevailing practice in the UK to treat only the site of the tumour, so to prevent radiation reaching his spine and other vital organs his chest was protected by a tailor made lead shield. Its positioning was pinpointed with a pattern of permanent tattoo marks on his body.

Treatment was suspended over Thanksgiving so, with his doctor's approval, we went away to Disneyland for a break with the whole family, including our then very young two granddaughters Sarah and Emily who, with their father and mother, were living in Chicago.

They say experience makes the man. I have unmatched admiration for Jamie's stoicism in facing this lethal challenge to his future and his well-being and his utter determination to beat his cancer. Una's and my distress at the diagnosis pales in comparison. When first told of his cancer we suddenly realised that we really knew nothing about the disease. For the next few days we searched vainly for information about types of cancer and the nature of Hodgkin's. At the prompting of my secretary, Judie Compher, we got hold of a copy of the *Merck Manual* from which we were able discover fuller details, which gave us great relief that Jamie's chances of a full and lasting recovery were very good. His doctor and oncologist were also superb in briefing us. Now, over a decade later, Jamie has beaten his cancer and made a complete recovery and enjoys a full life as a professional photographer undertaking projects in challenging places like the North Pole, Alaska and South America. I believe that we were fortunate that we were in the USA and had prompt access to excellent cancer specialists and latest technology and understanding of the disease when Jamie's cancer struck. I am also sure that the support of his sister, brother, and Una and me helped to complement his own courage and humour in facing down this disease. I believe it has given him a special appreciation of others who face similar challenges whether by way of illness or disability and a readiness to help where he can.

One day in the late 1980s, Chris Venkat, who worked for me as one of our part-time senior food technologists, came into my office and announced that he had decided to take up US citizenship and asked me if I would act as one of his supporters. Chris was also a Professor on the Faculty of Rutgers University near Washington DC and had been resident in the USA for well over a decade. Having ascertained that as a non-US citizen I could act in that capacity I readily agreed to his request. George Greer was to act as his other supporter.

A few weeks afterwards the appointed day arrived and I witnessed the very moving experience of helping someone become a citizen of the United States of America. Along with about fifty or sixty other individuals we assembled in the Federal building in Pittsburgh. Seated on the benches around us I noted small family groups. Some were obviously from far distant places – perhaps India, Asia, and the Caribbean – all of whom must have qualified to seek citizenship.

We rose as the Federal Judge in his black gown entered the Court Room. Seated, he welcomed everyone and then proceeded to describe the ceremony that all the aspiring US citizens would undergo in the next thirty minutes. He touched briefly on the history of the USA, its Government and values. Interestingly, he also drew everyone's attention to both the rights and the responsibilities that were there to be both enjoyed and respected as each person became a US citizen. Finally, he asked us all to rise and place in our hand the small US flag – the Stars and Stripes – that had been placed on each seat. He then pronounced: 'You are now citizens of the United States of America.' This was a very emotional moment for everyone present, both citizens and supporters. Tears flowed, hands were shaken and there was much hugging. It left a lasting impression on me and I reckon an even greater impression must have been left with the new citizens. I believe the UK has much to learn from the USA in the way in which it welcomes new citizens and makes them aware in a very lasting way of the rights and obligations that they take up as British citizens.

In the late 1800s, the sport of rowing flourished in Pittsburgh with some twenty boathouses gracing the shores of the three rivers and hundreds of rowing boats plying its waterways. Some of the better known boat clubs of those years included the Max Moorhead, the Chambers, the McKee, the Beck and the Undine. Rowing was mainly a working-class sport, and the clubs were often established by factory work crews and political coalitions. The boat clubs were also centres of social activities in their day – sponsoring picnics, parades, balls, and political rallies, as well as rowing competitions. On a typical summer evening, one might catch the strains of a brass or banjo band wafting across the water from the boathouse porch of the 'Third World Boys'.

On weekends, spectators would crowd the river banks and bridges, or clamber aboard river boats and railroad cars, to cheer their club favourites. Rowing was a professional sport in those days and betting was generally heavy. Given the high stakes at such events – and the often heavy consumption of alcohol – fights would occasionally break out in the crowd. More than once such affrays ended in a civil disturbance that could only be quelled by the intervention of the local constabulary.

However, the relentless expansion of steelmaking in Pittsburgh, which relied so heavily on water transportation, helped to bring the golden age of Pittsburgh rowing to a close. So too did the rise of new forms of popular entertainment: amusement parks, nickelodeons, boxing and baseball. The last rowing race on the Allegheny took place in 1887; nearly a century would pass before rowing boats in significant numbers again raced along Pittsburgh rivers.

By the early 1980s, steel making and related heavy engineering industries in Pittsburgh were nearing their demise and there were rumblings of interest in re-introducing rowing to Pittsburgh rivers now that they were virtually clear of heavy barge traffic. So in 1984, the Three Rivers Rowing Association (TRRA) was formed. A small committee comprising old rowers and others interested in the sport was established. Given my own past involvement in the sport I became a member of that committee, along with David F. Figgins, Chairman of a local Pittsburgh construction company who had rowed with Queen's University, Belfast, in his earlier days. It was obvious that if the emerging interest in the sport was to be capitalised upon, good facilities would have to be provided. This required fund-raising for the building of a boathouse and launching area, as well as comfort that it could be an economic enterprise on an on-going basis. By that time, each of Pittsburgh's four Universities had indicated a preparedness to pay rent for use of space in the proposed boathouse and, by opening it up to individual membership with annual dues, a satisfactory proforma was possible. Dave and I undertook the job as Joint Chairmen of a fund-raising campaign and by 1989, after some $700,000 had been raised, we opened probably the most modern boathouse then in the United States, housing some eighty craft along with exercise rooms, ergo machines and a social area. Contributors to the fund-raising had been individuals, local corporations, and importantly a $200,000 grant from the Pittsburgh Child Guidance Foundation which was to help TRRA teach rowing skills and values to inner city young people between the ages of 10 and 16. It also enabled us to encourage disabled and blind people to take up the sport. In 1987, TRRA organised and sponsored the first Ohio Head of the River Race on the Allegheny. This attracted a good number of crews from across the United States and was an encouraging beginning. In 1990, some 2,500 rowers participated in the Ohio Head, which also included International crews from the US and Great Britain. Thus, rowing was once again well established and TRRA, with a flourishing club membership, was able to operate successfully under the leadership of its newly appointed director, Mike Lambert.

In September 1992, I was invited to attend a breakfast meeting at the boathouse. Given my impending departure from Pittsburgh the following year, I had a suspicion that this breakfast might have something to do with that event. So it turned out to be and the inevitable speeches were made and I responded, underlining the great satisfaction that I had had in being a participant in the process of bringing rowing back to the City of Pittsburgh as a means of both showcasing the City and providing enormous enjoyment to young people of all backgrounds and ages. At that point I thought the proceedings were closed. However, we were all asked to move down to the boathouse forecourt and to my astonishment an eight-oared racing shell was brought out of the boathouse and I was asked to christen it – in the name of *R. Derek Finlay*. As I was pouring champagne over the bows I was aware – coming round the side of the boathouse – of the sound of pipes in the form of the Pittsburgh Pipes & Drums, dressed in full highland regalia. When they had finished playing I went over to the Pipe Major and congratulated him on his rendering of 'The Cock o' the North' and 'Scotland the Brave'. In reply he said, 'Say, that was nice of you – you're the first guy that's actually recognised anything we play!' The TRRA were gracious enough to ask me to maintain my connection as a founding governor – which I am still to this day. Since then a second boathouse and launch dock has been built and a further expansion up river is planned.

To me, the whole exercise in bringing this sport back to Pittsburgh and raising the funds necessary to do so, along with the active commitment of a wide range of local individuals and organisations in making it all happen, was a classic demonstration of how well a US

RDF christens the R. Derek Finlay *racing shell at the Three Rivers Rowing Association Boat House, Washington's Landing, Allegheny River, Pittsburgh, June 1993*

community can get to grips with and produce benefits for itself in a way that we haven't quite got round to being able to do in the same expeditious manner in the UK. Maybe it has to do with the greater feeling of obligation to contribute financially back into one's community and to give time and effort from otherwise very busy occupations. It was perhaps the most satisfying element of my non-Heinz life during our twelve years in Pittsburgh.

Shortly after my arrival in Pittsburgh in 1981, Tony O'Reilly discussed with me his wish to bring more international recognition to the city and the Heinz Company ideally involving business and academia. We kicked this idea around and together came up with the notion of a fellowship program to be focused on enabling carefully selected high potential individuals from developing nations who show early potential as future leaders of their countries in business, government and other professional sectors, and who have had had no exposure to the USA and its values, to spend a year's study and travel within the USA before resuming their careers in their home countries. Our hope was that such exposure would be a lasting experience for each Fellow that would help advance his or her career to positions of leadership and thus help spread US democratic values beyond US shores. Perhaps we were too enthusiastic in hoping that over time Heinz Fellows would become as well recognised as Harkness Fellows or Rhodes Scholars, but we believed the potential was there. I prepared a paper which we discussed with Dr Wesley Posvar, then President of the University of Pittsburgh, and Dr Burkhart Holzner, Head of the University Center for International Studies within the University. They both quickly warmed to our proposals that included a promise of an endowment from the Heinz Company Foundation to underpin the program. We secured their assurance that a suitable selection process could be put in place to search out candidates from likely countries and that fellows when chosen could choose subjects for study from the full range of courses available at the university.

Each Fellow was provided with a stipend and allowance for travel and was expected to deliver an academic paper at the end of his or her fellowship focusing on the findings of his or her studies and travels in the USA. To give more prominence to the program we agreed to sponsor an annual Heinz Fellowship Distinguished Lecture Series to be given by a person prominent internationally, so in 1983

The H. J. Heinz Company Foundation Program was launched and its first Fellow, Godwin Amuzu from the Republic of Ghana, arrived in Pittsburgh. The first Distinguished Lecture was delivered by Dr Garrett Fitzgerald, a past Taesoich of the Republic of Ireland. A man of express verbal delivery, the full enjoyment of his words was a distinct challenge for the majority of his distinguished audience. In the following ten years, seventeen Heinz Fellows experienced the program drawn from thirteen countries that included a wide spectrum of developing nations including India, China, Malaysia, Brazil, The Philippines, Pakistan, Croatia and Hungary.

Distinguished Lectures brought an array of current or ex world leaders as well as international statesmen to Pittsburgh. Their visits provided opportunities for local business, academic and civic leaders to meet them and exchange views. I found it fascinating to meet these personalities and observe them at close quarters. When I met Giscard d'Estaing, past President of France, in his hotel room he was giving final touches to his lecture notes. He took impish delight in telling me how he claimed to have outwitted Margaret Thatcher when there had been tension in agreeing the name for the unit of finance to be used in the fledgling years of the European Common Market. Apparently Mrs Thatcher had finally acquiesced in the use of the word 'ecu', the initials of the European Common Market. Giscard had then with Gallic satisfaction informed Mrs Thatcher that ecu was also the name of the old French currency! So France had prevailed again.

Given our involvement in Zimbabwe it was no surprise that in 1984 President Robert Mugabe came to Pittsburgh to deliver the lecture. It was notable that when Tony, President Posvar and I welcomed Mugabe on the platform, suddenly on the left his uniformed military ADC marched up to the podium, snapped to a noisy attention with polished boots, saluted and placed Mugabe's speech on the podium, moving off stage with equal military precision. He repeated the same procedure when Mugabe's speech was over.

We had always tried to ensure that the speaker had been briefed well ahead of his arrival to help him position his remarks. So imagine our dismay when Chancellor Helmut Schmidt's first words on arrival were, 'What is this program all about and what do you want me to say?'! His address was excellent – I suppose a demonstration of the politician's art of dealing with the unforeseen.

Tony and I had got to know Dr Henry Kissinger well as the result of many meetings we had had with him in New York from time to time. As well as being valuable, these occasions were akin to unique commentaries on world affairs drawing on his wide travels and experiences as US Secretary of State for Foreign Affairs under President Richard Nixon. During my travels in China his was always the name most quoted by Chinese officials in reference to his meetings with Chou En Lai when he and Nixon had made their memorable 1979 visit to China which launched the opening up to the west of that vast country. So his Heinz lecture was particularly memorable.

To me the most remarkable individual that I met as a result of the Heinz Lecture series was Nelson Mandela who came to Pittsburgh in 1991. He flew in from New York in our jet and I went to our hangar to meet him. The plane came to a gentle halt, engines died and in a moment the door opened, the steps wound down and out stepped Mandela. I shook his hand as he reached the ground and walked him across to our limo for the drive into Pittsburgh to meet my colleagues. Tall, slim and tastefully dressed in a dark suit, he sat beside me in the rear seat and we chatted as our driver made his way into the city. I thought to myself, 'The man beside me has spent twenty-six years of his life in jail – nearly half my lifetime. Yet he has no rancour, no apparent rage at his captors and their treatment of him over that time.' Even on that short journey his determination to achieve a better world for all in South Africa was evident, albeit combined with a great sense of humour.

We held a lunch in his honour in our offices. We had invited the CEOs of Pittsburgh's leading businesses and our own non-executive directors to join us. Henry Kissinger, who had not yet met Mandela, also came in especially from New York. You could not mistake the special feelings of all who attended that lunch as they were introduced to our guest. During lunch someone asked Mandela how he felt as he walked out of jail hand in hand with his wife Winnie. His reply was intriguing and illustrative of his attitude and his sense of humour. 'I had told the authorities that I wanted be driven out and did not want to walk out through the prison gates. However they insisted that we walk out. So as we started to walk and as I saw the crowds waiting beyond the gates, I whispered to Winnie: "I think I want to go back inside"!'

The time to deliver his lecture arrived. The platform party assembled off stage and we were placed in order waiting for the signal to go on. The University lecture theatre was packed and included a significant number of students many of whom were African Americans. We marched on to the stage to be greeted with a deafening roar of cheering and applause as Nelson Mandela acknowledged and enjoyed the audience's welcome. It went on for over five minutes before subsiding. I introduced the two new Heinz Scholars who were on the platform with us. Dr Wesley Posvar gave the University's words of welcome to Mandela and then Mandela stepped up to the podium to deliver his lecture. He had agreed beforehand to take a number of questions when he had concluded his lecture. The first question came from an African American student attired in jeans and headband. He challenged Mandela in fairly critical terms as to why he was on a platform with capitalist American businessmen who were only out to exploit South Africa and its people and should he not be pushing to help the African National Congress achieve its goal of the overthrow of the odious apartheid regime. Mandela's answer told me a great deal about the philosophy that would underlie his ascent to the Presidency of a South Africa freed from apartheid. 'You are wrong. For South Africa's people of all colours to develop their potential the country needs massive investment. We need the help of people and businesses represented here with me on this platform and elsewhere. They have got to be persuaded to provide the money, technology and skills. To be attracted to come they must be able to see the prospect of profit and a competitive return on their investment. So you must realise this and amend your views.' I think parts of his audience were chastened by his, to them, unexpected response. His words were reassuring to the businessmen present. The great rainbow promise that Mandela brought to his country when he became the first President of the new Rainbow South Africa got off to a wonderful start. I believe the tragedy is that his years of leadership were necessarily limited owing to his age when elected and that his successors may not be able to sustain the great hope and momentum that he engendered. Undoubtedly for me he was the most impressive individual that my business travels allowed me to meet.

So by 1991, the thoughts of Una and me turned to pondering whether we would return to the UK or stay in the USA when I finally retired from Heinz in 1993.

CHAPTER 12

Retirement – Numbers One and Two

WHEN UNA AND I ARRIVED IN PITTSBURGH in July 1981 the City was engaged in a massive programme of regeneration and redevelopment to bring more life back to the City and renew its cultural base. This programme arose from the recognition that the days of steel, coal and their associated industries were passing, if not already gone.

Pittsburgh glory days as one of the centres of America's industrial strength were waning fast. The US Steel Building where Heinz World Headquarters offices were located had in fact been named after the company whose founder, Andrew Carnegie, a Scot, is synonymous with the industry and its origins in Pittsburgh. His name is also synonymous with significant philanthropy and the Carnegie Trusts in both the USA and the UK continue to give away millions to worthy causes.

Pittsburgh was unusual in that many of its industries founding families, including names such as Frick, Mellon, Heinz and Westinghouse, contributed financial support to this transformation programme. Called the Allegheny Conference it also drew funds from the City Government, the Federal Government, Allegheny County, and local corporations. This combination achieved massive improvement in the City's infrastructure, including a highway programme to promote better access to the City. In the field of culture – Heinz Hall was refurbished, the Pittsburgh Public Theatre came to prominence, and latterly the Benedum Centre was redeveloped and opened as a centre for opera and ballet. New technology was encouraged and the City and its surrounding environment were able to capitalise on the academic strength represented by four leading Universities whose campuses were within the area. Pennsylvania State University operated four campuses. The University of Pittsburgh covered an array of disciplines with its thirty-five thousand student body. Carnegie Mellon, the smaller university, under the leadership of its President Richard (Dick) Cyert, who also sat on the Heinz Board as a non-executive director, established itself as a world leader in computers and information technology. Indeed it took great pleasure in beating the University of Texas in securing Federal financial support to develop a major new centre of expertise in information technology on a new site alongside the Allegheny River. To me it was significant that during the recession of the early 1980s, Pittsburgh came through that period with a lower rate of unemployment than the national average — quite the reverse of how the situation had been twenty years previously. So perhaps it was no surprise when Pittsburgh was designated the fourth largest corporate headquarters city in the United States and one of the most desirable areas for business development and academia. It had become a leading centre of medical research, its academic credentials were excellent and the surrounding environment and its ease of access to the bigger cities of New York and Washington contributed to its standing.

Over the twenty-five years that had spanned our two periods of residence in the US, in Chicago and Pittsburgh, we had made many good friends and our children by then had roots on both sides of the Atlantic.

Rory had married an American girl, MaryAnn Sokil, in New York in 1983 and by 1992 they had three super children, all showing great promise, and well-established in Evanston and subsequently Winnetka, Illinois. MaryAnn's family hailed from Eastern Europe and Rory was well embarked on a successful business career with the Wrigley Company, after taking a very well earned MBA at the Kellogg School of Business at North Western University in Chicago, by then the number one business school in the USA.

Fiona was in Hong Kong working as an Executive Search Consultant with Robert Friend & Associates where she carried out successful search projects as far afield as Australia as well as in Hong Kong. In 1993 she returned to the UK, acquired a Diploma at the Inchbald School of Design, established her own business and has become a very successful interior designer with clients in the UK and abroad. She is very happily married to Tom Lawrence who has built his practice as an acupuncturist and herbalist. Happily, Jamie was well on the way to full recovery from cancer and had resumed his studies at the University of Pittsburgh.

However, our own roots were tugging at both Una and me. Obviously we had considered the option of retiring in the USA. We both loved Scotland. We had many long-term friendships there from my early years in the Gordon Highlanders and subsequent Territorial Army service there. Her father's home had been in Angus and Una had been 'evacuated' to his family's home in Brechin near Montrose during the war years where she attended Arbroath High School. My 10-year service with the Gordons – Regular, National Service and the TA – meant that we had both made some of the most solid long-term friendships of our long life together.

My service with the Gordons in Malaya, covered elsewhere in this story, combined with my father's Scottish associations and of great friends, like John Rodger (who had recently retired as the veterinary surgeon at Crieff) and his wife Jean, David Macmillan and his wife Hilary, and Martin and Rona Cruickshank, who both had homes in Crianlarich, and Mike and Peggy Robson and Peter and Alison Graham in Aberdeen, all meant that we had a circle of friends to re-join in Perthshire and Aberdeenshire.

So, along with other factors, we decided that to Scotland we would retire. But where to start our search? Should we look in the north-east (Aberdeen and surrounding parts), the Montrose Basin near to Una's father's home? Or, more likely, where so many of our old chums lived in Perthshire, which offered good access to Edinburgh, Glasgow and London by road, rail or air.

Our original idea had been to find a good family home that would allow our children and grandchildren to visit and gather whenever they wanted to. Una was interested in an older property that would allow us to re-shape it to our own preferences and style. Early on in our search we saw a pleasant 300-year-old house near Montrose. Some restoration had been carried out but we decided this was not for us. But the idea of an older property with its own history was sown with us. On our behalf, Fiona had looked at a small castle in Argyll at the western end of Loch Fyne. At short notice we had asked a local surveyor to look it over for us. After we had decided that it was not for us, he mentioned that if we really wanted a castle there was one just coming on the market near Aberfeldy in Highland Perthshire. Its name was Grantully, originally a fifteenth century Z-shaped castle/fortified house. It had been in the ownership of branches of the same family – the Stewarts – for nearly six hundred years. Una, Fiona and Jamie went to see it and fell for the property. I was in Hong Kong at the time and received their fax to say they had viewed Grantully and 'you must see it – it's the place we've been looking for.'

On 30 April 1991 we gained entry and on 1 May the worldwide management team of the Heinz Company arrived by coach from Gleneagles where, by coincidence, our annual world headquarters conference was under way. I think many of my colleagues thought privately that we were quite mad to take on all that Grantully would entail to make it into a really comfortable home.

Suffice to say that nearly two and a half years later when I finally retired from Heinz, we had completed a major programme of renovation and refurbishment. All the work, including upgrading wiring and electrics, tanking to remove and protect the ground floor from persistent damp, installing central heating, connecting with mains gas and water, curtain-making, re-decoration throughout, carpet design by Una, weaving done by Sandy Grant (no relation) of Eskotex at his mill in Forfar, were all carried out superbly by local trades and craftsmen, who I think took great interest in being part of the team giving this old and historic building a new lease of life.

Given that we were still living in Pittsburgh, I persuaded a local surveyor and estate agent to act as our 'Clerk of Works'. Keith Moncrieff did a wonderful job of carrying out the total project plan that Una and I had drawn up with his help.

The result has given Una and me and our family a wonderful home in which to entertain friends from near and far and to enjoy our retirement. Subsequently I have often been asked what were the greatest pluses of my retirement from the Heinz Company after all the excitement of my years of work with the company. I think the primary bonus was to resume ownership of my diary and to cease travelling well over 300,000 air miles each year. As incomers we had generated a fair amount of curiosity as local rumour had it that an American businessman had taken over ownership of the castle and there was some apprehension as a consequence. However, despite our years in the USA, we had retained British accents and I was sure that that eased any possible anxiety that might have existed amongst what are now many good friends around us.

However, the peace and relative quiet that followed my departure from Heinz was to be relatively short-lived. In 1991 Hamish Morrison, then the Chief Executive Officer of the Scottish Council Development & Industry (SCDI), whom I had known for many years, approached me to ask whether I would be interested in becoming a non-executive director of a very well-known Scottish company called Dawson International plc, then a £400m vertically integrated cashmere manufacturer and international marketer of leading cashmere yarns and knitted garments. At that time it was the fourth or fifth largest textile business in the UK, with ownership of such well-known brands as Ballantyne, Barrie, Pringle and Braemar. In the mid 1980s Dawson had also acquired Morgan Knitting Mills, the largest manufacturer in the USA of thermal underwear based in Hometown, Pennsylvania. This purchase was an integral part of its strategy to participate more directly in the US marketplace and limit the risks associated with its other business's reliance on world raw cashmere prices and the increasing power of the Chinese producers of the raw fibre as they sought to broaden into yarn manufacture, knitting, and marketing of finished knitted garments.

Heinz policy was to allow its executive directors to take up two non-executive directorships, subject to approval of the Chairman and Chief Executive Officer. To me Dawson seemed an interesting opportunity to bring to bear my own extensive international experience of foreign markets and operating in a very well managed international corporate environment. I met the Chairman, Ronald Miller, in New York where he provided me with more background on the company and its then strategy.

In the mid to late 1980s the fashion for quality cashmere knitted garments still flourished. The twin-set, pioneered by Pringle, held on to a position among discerning buyers both at home and abroad. Ballantyne held a premier position in the luxury markets of the emerging Asian economies in Hong Kong, Singapore, Taiwan, and the more mature markets in Japan and the USA. Despite its association with Nick Faldo in his heyday, the Pringle brand had suffered from its identification with the unruly world of the English football fan amongst whom a Pringle Argyle jersey seemed to be the garment of choice and seemed to feature particularly on TV coverage of bad behaviour by soccer fans. Needless to say that did not produce good public relations for the brand.

Despite expensive and largely futile efforts to replicate in Scotland the breeding of the variety of goat that produces the delicate outer fibre in its coat as an added protection to surviving the intense cold of Inner Mongolia in its homeland in Northern China, the de-hairing (cleaning) of the raw fibre had concentrated over the years in the UK. Joseph Dawson who gave his name to Dawson International had developed the process at his Yorkshire base to produce the finest fibres for onward carding, spinning, and knitting.

The world of cashmere is small: dominated by Scottish, Italian, Japanese and Chinese knitters, drawing a high proportion of their raw materials from Dawson International either as de-haired cashmere fibre or spun dyed yarns to be knitted into garments designed by those companies. Dawson had built a commanding position in those markets as a leading international buyer of raw fibre and its yarn subsidiary, Todd & Duncan (T&D), based at Loch Leven Mills at Kinross, was probably the world's pre-eminent yarn spinner. T&D had been the foundation stone of Dawson International when Sir Alan Smith, its then managing director, used the company as a base for acquiring Ballantyne, Pringle, and a number of smaller but well-known knitted brands such as Barrie, Braemar and McGeorge. Each of these relatively small companies operated its own manufacturing and design capability and ran independent sales forces selling through different agents in Europe, Asia and the US. On his retirement in the early 1980s, Sir Alan appointed Ronald Miller, then Chief Accountant, as his successor.

By the end of the 1980s, Chinese knitters had carved out a significant export business in cheaper, lower quality, lower priced cashmere garments, coincident with lower raw cashmere prices. Dawson responded to this pressure in three ways. First, steps were taken to rationalise several of its small brand businesses into one organisation – to be known as Dawson International United Brands. Next, it launched a strategy to build Pringle into a major £100m international brand to challenge and try to emulate the success of Dunhill. As part of that effort some twelve retail outlets were opened on the Continent, thus taking Pringle into the different world of retail operation. The product range was extended dramatically beyond knitted garments into jewellery, women's dresses, perfume, leatherwear etc; in fact well beyond Pringle's traditional line of knitted garments. Its third response was to establish a foreign joint venture with King Deer, a fast growing integrated cashmere business in China.

In the USA in the 1980s and 1990s the retail giant Wal-Mart was increasing its geographic coverage and dominance in many grocery and non-food categories. Significantly, along with K Mart and Target, the two other major discount retailers in the USA, they dominated the thermal underwear market both in the lower priced 'long john' segment and increasingly the higher margin Duofold product. Morgan held dominant shares in these market segments but in a sense this dominance was its greatest risk as 'it had nowhere else to go' to develop higher margin alternative sales outlets. Its No. 1 competitor, Hanes, was owned by Sarah Lee, the US food and textile multi-national that I had known well from my Heinz days. To service the short two-months selling cycle between December and January production was year round so that inventory build-up was significant with its associated financial risk should winter weather moderate or the pressures of just in time (JIT) exerted by Wal-Mart increase that risk. Morgan's premier line Duofold also held a special niche in the high-tech end of the thermal market but by far the largest part of Morgan's production was sold in downmarket chains like K Mart and Target, in addition to Wal-Mart.

By 1993 these pressures were building up. The rationalisation of Dawson's smaller brands had yielded some savings arising from factory closures and redundancies. However the strategy had not taken sufficient account of the significant difficulties inherent in trying to rationalise, change or rupture long-standing agency relation-ships where the loyalty to these individual brands was long-standing and there were legal/contractual issues that inevitably arose.

Combined with the first signs of the 'dumbing down' of mainstream fashion in the 1990s and the arrival of cheap casual fleece garments, Dawson's performance came under severe pressure and profits were severely squeezed to the point of disappearance. In 1993, Dawson had made a £40m rights offer with the objective of investing in the Pringle expansion strategy. By late 1994 it was clear that this strategy was failing. Sales volumes were significantly below budget; unsold garment inventories were piling up, as well as stocks of the other sourced Pringle lines. In addition, the venture into retail store operation was demonstrating that it is an area of business which requires managers with solid successful retail selling and marketing experience, where manufacturing skills do not on their own bring success. Many of the stores were clearly unprofitable.

Needless to say, as non-executive directors Ronald Alexander, Ann Burdus and I were deeply concerned at the worsening picture. Early in 1995 we decided that radical action had to be taken given the loss in shareholder value and the collapse of the share price. My own non-executive colleagues pressed me to lead the change in senior management and take over the chairmanship from Sir Ronald Miller, who had received his Knighthood two years earlier.

I approached this mission with very mixed feelings. Una and I had settled well into Grantully and I was enjoying the pleasures of a less hectic lifestyle with little or no long-haul flying round the world, and a diary that I could call my own. I was also taking advantage of time to pursue other personal interests. I was still deputy chairman of Olivine Industries, the Heinz joint venture affiliate in Zimbabwe, which, along with my non-executive role at Dawson's, made a very satisfying and workable commitment.

Effecting the top management changes needed – the resignation of the Chairman, Sir Ronald Miller, and the Chief Executive, Nick Kuenssberg – forced me to deal for the first time in nearly forty years of management experience with the phenomenon called management contracts. In common with most senior executives in US companies at the time, I had never had or required such a contract in nearly thirty years as a senior executive. I had always operated in an environment where rich rewards flowed from a job well done and where shareholders were equally well rewarded. In the case of failure or below par performance, executives moved on with some recognition, maybe with a part or all of an annual bonus, or several months' salary, and then found new employment having set aside over time sufficient financial resource to bridge the period up to securing other employment. My terms as a Senior Vice President at Heinz were in fact based on six months' notice.

My expectation therefore was that after the difficult discussions surrounding their departure, and particularly in view of the crisis in Dawson's performance 'an American style' departure would be appropriate. However, Dawson's company lawyers advised me in no uncertain terms that my proposed approach would put the company in breach of the individual's contract with the company, which would probably result in legal proceedings being taken against the company and that I and my colleagues' time would be taken up by extensive court action. Consequently negotiated settlements with appropriate mitigation were reached.

Among my first actions when I was appointed Chairman in March 1995 was to sanction the closure of the Pringle factory at Arbroath in eastern Scotland with the loss of 300 local jobs. In contrast those employees received rather smaller payouts for the loss of their jobs.

In ensuing years this issue has come under intense scrutiny by the Gods of corporate governance and pressure has resulted in the reduction of most management contracts to a maximum of 12 months.

I am probably naïve in this matter but I would still argue strongly against the use of contracts at all, except perhaps in the case of change of control. Senior management is and should be a high-risk occupation if companies are to grow and take measured steps to improve shareholder value. I have no problem with high rewards for success but on the downside there should be little or no reward for failure. Otherwise the market-based capitalist system becomes virtually risk-free for senior managers and, indeed, opens up a peculiar career path of accumulating wealth by failure. Of even greater importance, it does the reputation of corporate business great damage socially and politically and plays into the hands of those sections of the community who wish to denigrate the system and those politically motivated opponents of the free enterprise business system, which is still, I believe, the surest foundation of wealth generation for the community at large.

Although offered, I did not accept a contract as Chairman of Dawson and excluded myself from all benefits.

I was fortunate to be able to call on two Dawson managers as my turn around team: Peter Forrest, then Managing Director of the Fibres and Yarns Division, had joined Dawson in 1991 as Corporate Development Director bringing a wealth of industry experience from his years at Courtaulds and nearly nine years in Italy working in the jeans business, with the added benefit of fluency in Italian; George Fairweather, Finance Director, had joined the company in 1990 from Dixon's where he had seen service in the USA.

Shortly after taking post I made an important discovery that I believe is characteristic of the risks that can be run by non-executive directors of public companies where they are reliant on the accuracy and integrity of the information provided to them when taking key decisions at Board level. My discovery was the fact that financial systems of control and the underlying ingredients of the management information that reached the Board were in many cases flawed, inadequate or inaccurate. So one of the first tasks already being addressed by George Fairweather was the establishment of financial controls across the many Dawson companies where common usage, definition, etc. could bring accuracy to the presentation of management reports and profit forecasts. Of equal, perhaps greater, immediate importance was the need to brief all our employees and bring home to each and every one the gravity of the situation and the need for urgent radical action to restore profitability. I tried to set out our goals clearly, along with the reasons for the steps that needed to be taken – with the help of a video shown to all employees.

By 1995 the external environment for cashmere had changed quite dramatically from the lusher years of the early 1980s. The Chinese had made serious inroads into the lower value knitted garments market and developed strong export markets in the US and Japan particularly. Their increased requirement for raw fibre put upward pressure on prices and Joseph Dawson's strong position and influence in that market came under severe strain. The growing luxury brand markets in Asia from where much of the growth had come became hostages to economic downturn. However despite these negatives, Dawson held ground in 1995/6. My underlying concern was to develop a strong balance sheet with lower gearing and a positive cash flow to see the company viably through the turn around exercise. We were making reasonable headway during 1995/6. But then economic downturn almost shut down the Asian luxury brand markets. In 1996/7 sterling continued to strengthen against the franc, lire, and deutschmark, the primary currencies of our European export markets. Thus in the space of six months this adverse exchange rate movement amounted to almost a 30 per cent increase in the delivered price of UK produced garments into those markets. In addition Italian knitters, our primary European competitors in Asian markets, were pricing in lire at a similar discount to sterling. Taken together these factors forced emerging profit back into loss.

Our search for a Chief Executive Officer (CEO) had failed to yield sufficiently attractive candidates, so in early 1998 Peter Forrest was appointed CEO and Paul Munn was confirmed as Finance Director, having been appointed in succession to George Fairweather who had left the company in 1997 to join Harrison Crossfields in London. Paul had joined Dawson from BUPA as Corporate Development Manager in which position he had showed great promise. I was comfortable with his appointment and his steadiness under fire.

In 1997, I had informed the Board of my intention to retire in 1998, so in October of that year I handed over the non executive chairmanship of Dawson International plc to Ian Irvine, then also Chairman of Capital Radio. So I started out on retirement number two with a firm view that this would be the last one.

As I look back on this experience several years later, I believe a superior strategy might have been to break up the company at the time of the 1995 debacle. Shareholders could have been repaid although serious loss would still have resulted. But more value might have been placed in the hands of shareholders than the outcome reached by 1998. In human terms of the lost jobs and skills arising from the turnaround strategy, I think the outcome would have been little different. The UK's position as a base for textile manufacture has been declining for the last half century and I believe will continue to shrink. To succeed it requires the combination of the latest technology, transferable skills, and a low wage workforce. These conditions are ideal candidates for developing countries (as indeed the UK was in the mid to late 1800s when textiles were a large employer and a major export industry for the UK).

The UK's strength is still in design which, given the coming of IT, enables those skills to be still based in the UK and downloaded to anywhere in the world where low-cost manufacture is available or can be developed. We demonstrated this strategy successfully at Dawson in our Chinese joint venture which enabled computer designs developed in Hawick in the Scottish Borders to be transferred 'down the line' to Luyuan Dawson in China where, using the latest Japanese computer-operated knitting machinery and well trained lower cost personnel, high quality garments could be produced and sold to leading US retailers like Nordstrom, Nieman Marcus, and Saks at competitive prices and decent margins, incidentally avoiding the quota restrictions on exports out of the UK into the US that prevailed at that time under the terms of the World Multi-Fibre Agreement.

It is notable too that several successful cashmere businesses are either relatively small with well promoted brands and virtually no manufacturing assets or privately owned and therefore not subject to the public glare attaching to a publicly quoted company which, to a company in Dawson's situation, provided no real advantages – virtually no market in the stock and unable to raise finance given the unattractively low share price over the period.

I believe that Ralph Lauren have developed the most successful strategy for the future of textiles and fashion garments. I think it has taken that business nearly twenty years to establish a position of pre-eminence and the lessons learned I believe are worthy of note by others in the industry. This successful international brand has followed a dedicated strategy under its founder Ralph Lauren characterised by

- No manufacturing assets in developed higher labour cost markets
- Designer skills located in a place of high fashion and cultural creativity, e.g. New York
- World class sourcing operations, able to 'cherrypick' products from anywhere in the world, searching for manufacturing quality and delivery service at lowest cost
- Well honed distribution, merchandising and selling skills working through a combination of licensees and/or agents with some directly owned flagship retail stores in leading cities such as New York and London
- Targeted use of well sited 'Factory Outlet' stores, for example outside New York or Bicester near Oxford in the UK, to move slower moving discounted lines and thus reduce inventory build up.

The result from the above combination is greater flexibility to react to and lead changes in fashion with much shorter lead times, thus enabling marketing and sales promotion skills to be brought to bear with little or no fixed manufacturing assets to distract management's focus on design and marketing.

To say the least, my three-year service as Chairman of Dawson International was interesting, stimulating, and also frustrating. Having experienced so many years as a senior executive in one of the best-managed multi-nationals in the food industry, the world of textiles and luxury brands offered many contrasts. The application of computers to design skills was, to me, amazing. I remember watching one of our designers demonstrate how sitting at a computer he was able to create a garment on the screen. He created its shape, its knitting characteristics, colours, and the right selection and mix of yarns. The finished design was then transferred to a floppy disk, which was in turn transferred to a computer-operated knitting machine (incidentally of Japanese manufacture – the home of the latest technology). Within a matter of minutes the panels of the garment were knitted and ready for final assembly, and one operator could control up to ten or more such machines.

HRH The Princess Anne opens the Pringle Chinese Garden, The Botanical Gardens,
Edinburgh, 1997

This technology was also a major step in shortening the tradition-
ally long lead-time between conventional design and factory production of actual garments. It shortened the period between a trade
buyer agreeing a design and placing his order and putting it into
production. Thus these decisions could be made closer to the likely
time of sale with the benefit of the latest fashion trend input. This
meant lower inventory held for shorter periods with lower capital
tied up. However financial risk is increased at this stage because until
a range of garments is actually offered for sale in a retail store and
subjected to the consumers' verdict, there is no certainty as to
whether the range is 'cold', in which case remaining inventory
becomes slow moving or surplus and must be deeply discounted and
incur severe financial loss or write off, or 'hot' when resources need
to be directed to sharply increased production.

I have often characterised success in the manufacture and marketing of high fashion garments as high stakes gambling. For example,
unlike the relative steadiness of daily-consumed food items – for

example a 15 oz can of Heinz Baked Beans – which around the seasons roll off retail shelves with only occasional ups and downs, the high fashion industry still lives or dies by its success or failure with its spring and autumn collections and its ability to modify its main repeat lines in line with fashion trends. Forecasting design and fashion trends and generating inventory to back sales is at least six months ahead of actual sale to the consumer. His, or mostly her, tastes are fickle and changeable. Get it right, as Pringle unwittingly did with its Argyle woven jerseys in the 70s and 80s, and sales are buoyant; get it wrong as Pringle did in its over zealous expansion strategy in the early 90s, and the penalties are life threatening – as Pringle discovered.

My frustrations were several. The uncertainty of the trading environment which hit Dawson just as the turn-around strategy was starting to yield positive results was tough for all of us. The underlying internal financial surprises as George Fairweather struggled to revamp the financial control systems and improve the flow of consistent, accurate, management information were not what I had been accustomed to, perhaps spoiled by the quality of Heinz control systems. As I have commented elsewhere, I do believe that lady luck can also help or hinder success in business. For us at Dawson she provided no help. Between 1996 and 1997, sterling strengthened by nearly 30 per cent against the deutschmark, the lire, and the franc. To a business such as Dawson, which relied heavily for its recovery on a friendly, encouraging, economic environment for continued growth in luxury products, an effective price increase of that magnitude in local currency for a business relying so heavily on exports for its recovery, these were serious body blows. It immediately offered our Italian competitors a major price advantage, which, combined with their undoubted design skill, increased competition for our luxury brands such as Ballantyne – both on the Continent and in important Asian markets. Throughout the roller-coaster ride of those times my prime financial concern was to ensure the maintenance of a strong balance sheet still able to generate cash and to hold gearing well below 20 per cent, which put us in acceptable standing with our solid Scottish bankers.

I must also pay tribute to the Dawson workforce over these hectic years. Throughout the necessary closures of factories, redundancy programmes, and significant change in working practices, we lost no days to strike action. Peter Forrest and his management teams did yeoman work in giving regular briefing sessions to all our employees and we insisted always that any major change, staff reduction, or factory closure, was communicated firstly to the workers affected. Politicians and the press and TV followed, well handled by our capable Director of Communications, Fiona Scott.

So by October 1998, I had retired for the second time in five years, this time, however with the firm resolve to say 'no' in future to any friends bearing non-executive directorships. It strengthened my resolve to say no to the several approaches that I received in subsequent years. It seemed to me that the risk/reward equation had become too weighted in the wrong direction. I am not surprised that in current times fewer managers of talent and experience are available to the head-hunters as candidates for PLC Chairmen or Non Executive Directorships.

CHAPTER 13

Dues

I N 1994, I RECEIVED A TELEPHONE CALL from a very dear friend from my Emmanuel days, Owain Howell. A Welshman and one-time passing good rugby player and cricketer, his opening words in his Welsh lilt were, 'If you have a moment I think you will be interested in what I have to tell you.' He had got my interest, and he went on to describe how in recent years he had been a member of a panel of outsiders helping sixth-form students at Downside School to sharpen up their interview skills as they approached University or looked for employment post their school years. He had been invited to join this panel several years before by the Abbot of Downside whom he had got to know well.

At daily prayers in the monastery the Abbot always offered remembrance to two flyers killed in a flying accident. Apparently for many years he had tried to discover the Christian name of one of those two flyers. I said to Owain, 'Is the Abbot's name Jebb?' 'Yes,' Owain replied, 'Father Philip Jebb.' I said, 'He must be Hilaire Belloc's grandson, and the flyers' names must have been Roger Forder, DFC of Selwyn College, Cambridge, and my brother Douglas Finlay, DFC of Emmanuel College, Cambridge.' Father Jebb — the same age as myself — had been at his family's home at Shipley near Horsham in Sussex on 23 August 1948. It was a sunny day and he and his younger brother were chopping wood in an outhouse in the grounds. In a subsequent letter to me he said:

> As my brother and I were working in the shed at 1 p.m. we heard above the noise of the considerable wind the sound of a Tiger Moth engine going at full power, and we came out to look. I think it had probably been doing a loop, but was too low to complete it as it was going down wind, and so not going fast enough through the air. By the time we saw it, it was in a very steep dive, and having watched the whole of the Battle of Britain from this house I was convinced that it could not pull out. But I did not realise how small a Tiger Moth was and I thought that it would crash a couple of fields away, well off to the right of the house. We both started running when it crashed

almost beside us, leaving the two bodies at our feet. Both were killed instantly and did not survive the impact.

Looking back on it, I suspect that the dive was steeper than it needed to have been, although in fact this was probably intentional on the part of the pilot (I do not know which of the two this was), in order not to hit the house. If they had, it would inevitably have caught fire, and both my parents, my younger brother and my grandfather would very probably have been killed as well.

Owain had kindly spoken first to my daughter Fiona to check whether I would wish to stir memories from so long ago as he had been aware of my brother's time at Emmanuel. She thought he should contact me. So, he sketched all the above to me on that telephone call and said would I like to meet Father Jebb, or was the tragedy now so far in the past and therefore best left unstirred? Father Jebb had told Owain that he would be happy to tell me of his experience on that day and of his desire to learn more of the two flyers that he remembered in his daily prayers.

This was to be a very special moment for me. Deep down, despite a loving wife and family, over the years I had missed the companion-ship of my older brother as after his return from prison camp in May 1945, we were starting to get to know each other better and I was becoming less of the proverbial small brother. I had often wondered how my life might have been different if he had lived.

I met Owain at Bath Railway Station and we drove to Downside Abbey. It was another sunny day when I shook hands with Philip Jebb. After a lunch in the monastery with the Benedictine Brothers seated at bare refectory tables, silent as is their custom except for the voice of one of the brothers reading aloud to all of us from a novel, he took me to his rooms where he described in detail what he had witnessed on 23 August 1948. I was able to describe to Philip Jebb the highlights of my brother's life and the values he had lived by, and to provide the piece of missing information – his Christian name, Douglas. He emphasised to me how his family had always offered thanksgiving that the plane had not crashed on their home. He was certain that this was due solely to the efforts of the pilot to avoid the house – sadly to crash fatally in their gardens.

To me this meeting was quite unique. In the Air Force enquiry that had followed the deaths of Roger Forder and my brother, the Air Ministry had insisted that there was no fault found in the Tiger

Moth's engine or other parts of the plane and that, thankfully, their deaths had been immediate. For my father, and less so myself, there had always been a lingering doubt that with two experienced wartime bomber pilots, this crash was more likely to have been the result of some structural problem with the aeroplane. That's a piece of the story that probably will always be left unresolved. However, to me the unique opportunity to talk the events of that day through with a person of my own age who had been an eye witness to my brother's death in the detail that he provided enabled me to achieve closure, for which I was terribly grateful.

In 1991 there was a major fundraising campaign to improve the infrastructure and facilities of Emmanuel College. It was led by the then Master, Norman St John Stevas, otherwise known as Lord St John of Fawsley. Una and I decided to make a significant contribution to the campaign with a further contribution being made by the H.J. Heinz Company Foundation. In making it, I had enquired of the Development Director whether it might be possible for my brother's name to be remembered in some way in the College. Some time went by. Then I was approached by the College with an unusual but very thoughtful idea. The Master believed that the College needed somewhere where it could record past achievements and maintain part of its archives. The suggestion was that this should be set up in the Junior Common Room beneath the Harvard Scholar's Rooms in Old Court and be called 'The Museum of College Life'. Would I agree to the museum being named after my brother? I thought this was a wonderful idea and agreed immediately. After further discussions with the Master and Dr Michael Rickard, then Curator, the details were agreed. Early in 1995 the Master phoned me to tell me that HRH The Prince of Wales had graciously agreed to conduct the opening ceremony. So, on Friday 22 September 1995 as recorded in the Court Circular of the day:

> The Prince of Wales honoured the Master and Fellows of Emmanuel College by visiting the College yesterday and opening the new Museum of College Life in Old Court. The Museum is named in honour of Flight Lt. Douglas Finlay DFC, a member of the College who died in 1948. Mr & Mrs Derek Finlay and other members of the family were present.
>
> Afterwards, the Prince of Wales visited the Queen's Building opened by the Queen in April and Sir Michael and Lady Hopkins, its

Architects, were present. Later he attended a reception when Lord St John of Fawsley, Master of the College, presented Fellows and Junior Members of the College, the Vice-Chancellor Elect, Professor Alec Broers, other Heads of Houses and representatives of the University were among those present.

It was another memorable day. Rory had flown in specially from America and joined Una, me, Fiona and Jamie for the occasion. Along with Michael Rickard we assembled in the Museum to await HRH. He duly arrived accompanied by the Master, the Vice-Chancellor Elect and several other College Fellows. I think Lord St John was a little surprised when Prince Charles gave me a smile of recognition and we shook hands and I showed him the small exhibit that we had assembled, including my brother's POW logbook, his Stalag Luft III metal name tag with its prisoner number and one or two other items.

There was a particular reason for that smile of recognition. In 1991 it had already become obvious that under the Options for Change Policy inaugurated by Tom King MP (the then Minister of Defence and also a contemporary of mine at Emmanuel), that the Gordon Highlanders were probably going to lose their independence and be either disbanded or merged with one of the three remaining Highland Regiments. A major campaign was launched in the regimental areas of north-east Scotland to try to save the Regiment from at worst extinction or amalgamation. As time went by it became increasingly certain that the Regiment would find itself merged with the Queen's Own Highlanders (itself the result of a merger thirty-one years previously of the Seaforth and Cameron Highlanders). At this point the Colonel of the Regiment, Lt. General Sir Peter W. Graham, KCB, CBE decided that a serious effort would be mounted to make the Regimental Museum in Aberdeen a focal point for preserving the memory and heritage of the Gordons. A major appeal was launched to raise sufficient funds to purchase the Museum site at Viewfield Road in Aberdeen from the Ministry of Defence and push ahead with transforming the existing museum into a viable ongoing business and an attractive location for visitors from far and wide. As I was still resident in Pittsburgh, Sir Peter asked me to chair the North American Committee, which I was happy to do.

The Regiment's Honorary Colonel in Chief was HRH The Prince of Wales, Duke of Rothesay. He was very supportive as the campaign developed and Una and I had cause to meet him at functions at Birkhall and the Town House in Aberdeen. So hence the reason why there was a smile of recognition from the Prince when he arrived to open the Douglas Finlay Museum of College Life at Emmanuel College.

Under Sir Peter Graham's leadership the Gordon Museum in Aberdeen has been successful and is a worthy addition to the tourist attractions of Aberdeen City, as well as providing a centre of gravity for Old Gordons and keeping alive the heritage and values of service embodied in the Gordon Highlanders, described by Sir Winston Churchill during his travels in South Africa during the Boer War as 'the finest regiment in the British Army'.

Having spent such a large part of my adult life associated with or resident in the USA both as a business executive and as a member of thriving communities such as Chicago and Pittsburgh, I had become much more aware of that element of American life and its values that just expects that public service and philanthropy – on whatever scale – is the challenge to every citizen within his or her means.

This philosophy manifests itself in many ways. In my case my service on the Boards of the Pittsburgh Symphony Society, Mercy Hospital, the Pittsburgh Public Theatre, as Chairman of the Board of Visitors at the School for International Studies at the University of Pittsburgh, as a Governor of the Three Rivers Rowing Association and as a Trustee of the H.J. Heinz Company Foundation, gave me insights into the myriad ways in which individuals from all sections of society contributed their time, skills and, yes, their money to help and support the arts, their communities and beneficial social projects aimed at less well off sections of their communities. This 'volunteer-ism' and sense of personal obligation to the community contrasts still, in my view, with the prevailing notion of the all-pervasive welfare state that still persists in some sections of the chattering classes and the political elite in the UK and in many other European countries. The latter philosophy over time saps individual initiative, generates dependency by the citizen on the state, and ultimately is unaffordable without massive increases in government expenditure, which hit hardest the wealth generating sectors of the community on which the growth in national prosperity ultimately relies.

Cynics will say that the USA is an uncaring society because it lacks the extensive social programmes that characterise the welfare state model. I believe such views are wrong and misguided. They overlook the essential point of difference – the primacy of the individual citizen in the USA versus the State and or the Federal Government. The USA is not a perfect society but so far it has generated a higher standard of living for the majority of its citizens that any other large economy. And every citizen, no matter what his or her status in life, can aspire to and often does achieve his or her share of 'the American Dream'.

So, in the closing stages of my business career I had established a personal goal of 'paying my dues' to the three institutions that had not only given me my start in life but had also provided experiences that had shaped my values and the friendships that I have been privileged to enjoy over forty and in some cases fifty years. The Douglas Finlay Museum at Emmanuel enabled me to repay a debt of gratitude to that institution.

My military service as a National Service Platoon Commander in Malaya with the 1st Battalion the Gordon Highlanders under active service conditions had given me – like I believe many others – an unparalleled experience which made me much more aware of and sensitive to the tougher side of life. So I was glad to have the opportunity to help in the fundraising campaign for the Gordon Highlanders Museum and to ensure that the Museum's kitchen is properly equipped to provide first-class fare for the corporate dinners and conferences that are now an important part of the Museum's income.

My Asian experience also left me with a fascination with that part of the world that I am sure I was able to exploit on behalf of the Heinz Company in carrying forward our growth strategy around the Pacific Rim and in the Indian Sub Continent. This effort has left a legacy that should develop into strong positions for Heinz in those growing markets in the years ahead.

The third debt of gratitude that I owed was to my old school, Kingston Grammar School. That institution with its academic origins in the thirteenth century and its re-founding by Elizabeth I in 1561 had given me a superb education in my formative years. So I got great pleasure out of opening a new Department of Art & Technology at the school in 1991, which now goes under the name 'The Finlay Gallery'.

In 2002, I had completed a seven year term as a Governor of the school and was on the point of retiring from the Governing Body.

My family – the real point of my story. (L to r) Jamie, Emily, Rory, Fiona, RDF, Una, William, Sarah, Tom, MaryAnn

Jamie and Geneviève on their wedding day, 6 May 2006

During the previous three years of that service I had led a Fundraising Appeal, which had equipped the school with an up-to-date Information Technology computer network and also provided students with a modern language laboratory. The appeal's final goal had been to provide the school with a second new astro turf international standard hockey pitch, to help maintain the school's unparalleled pre-eminence in the sport. With contributions from the Old Kingstonian Association, the Old Kingstonian Hockey Club, gifts from others including myself and a welcome grant from school funds, the pitch was constructed with the inclusion of tennis courts and a basketball area.

It came as a great surprise to me when John Elvidge, Chairman of the Governing Body and like myself an old Kingstonian, contacted me to inform me that the Governing Body wanted to put my name on the new pitch and would I perform the opening ceremony at the school playing fields opposite Hampton Court Palace. I appreciated greatly this unexpected gesture. So my last act as a Governor was to declare the Finlay Pitch ready for its first exhibition game, ably supported by Fiona and Tom, her husband, and Jamie.

An American football game is divided into four quarters. I well remember Tony O'Reilly coming into my office one day in Pittsburgh and, after exchanging some views on a particular topic, commented that we were both 'in the second half'. I was then 58 and Tony was 54. My reply was to correct Tony. 'No, actually we're probably in the final quarter!'

So I can now look back on a satisfying life that has brought Una and me, our children Fiona and husband Tom, Rory and his wife MaryAnn, Jamie and Geneviève, our new French Canadian daughter-in-law, and our grandchildren, Sarah, Emily and Will, a lot of fun, wonderful experiences and the wherewithal to enjoy life to the full. The whole enterprise would not have been possible without the unstinting support of my beloved wife Una. It may sound hackneyed to say so in these modern times, but she is still my sweetheart. I have truly been a lucky man as I can now look forward to 'ten to take her home' – the Cox's call as we spurted to put in the vital ten strokes to cross the finishing line – hopefully always ahead of our opponents!

Index